How Capitalism Works

How Capitalism Works

Pierre Jalée

Translated by Mary Klopper

Monthly Review Press
New York and London

Originally published in Paris, France, by François
Maspero under the title L'exploitation capitaliste,
copyright ©1974 by Librairie François Maspero

Library of Congress Cataloging in Publication Data

Jalée, Pierre.
    How capitalism works.

    Translation of L'exploitation capitaliste.
    Includes bibliographical references.
    1. Marxian economics.   2.Capitalism.
I. Title.
HB97.5.J3613   335.4'12   77-80313
ISBN 0-85345-416-7

First Modern Reader Paperback Edition
First Printing

Monthly Review Press
62 West 14th Street, New York, N.Y. 10011
47 Red Lion Street, London WC1R 4PF

Manufactured in the United States of America

Contents

6   *Contents*

1
Introduction

In recent years I have often been asked: "Can you tell us of a book or pamphlet which offers a clear and simple analysis of the capitalist economic and social system—which penetrates its mechanisms and presents a concise overall view?" This question has arisen at lecture-discussions, seminars, and in private conversations. It has been posed as often by workers as by students, as often by intellectual petty bourgeois as by activists in radical organizations. The people asking these questions already had a critical view of the capitalist system, however intuitive or limited this view might be. They felt the need of easily accessible but scientific information, not only for the satisfaction of learning, but to put political or trade union action on a sound basis.

The question was obviously, if not always explicitly, about a good popular *Marxist* work. It is notable nowadays that many people who still have instinctive doubts about the materialist philosophy nevertheless turn to it for an economic, social, and political critique of capitalism. I did not know of any such book or pamphlet. The few attempts in this direction seem to me both incomplete and dogmatic, and too abstract and academically worded to please my inquirers. Although I may not be the most suitable person for such a task, that is why I eventually undertook it myself.

Thus, it is the purpose of this book to be accessible to any person who has had no preparation in its field. Yet it is my ambition to give a coherent view of capitalist society, which omits nothing essential, but is restricted to the fundamental structure and mechanisms. I have taken pains not to betray the Marxist analysis by condensing it, and to avoid *dishonest* simplification on the pretext of writing for beginners. It is clear that these considerations cannot be entirely reconciled, and I was aware at the start that success could at best be partial. I shall be satisfied, however, if the reader closes the book feeling better equipped for the struggle against a system that must now be overthrown. That was my sole purpose in writing it.

2
Production:
How and With What?

Let us consider the workers in any factory, for instance a steel mill: they bring iron ore and coke together at high temperatures to produce various kinds of iron and steel. Today the workers go to collect their wages—that is, a certain number of dollars. This raises a host of questions. What do these wages represent? They are generally believed to represent the workers' labor, but we shall see that it is not as simple as that. Who pays the wages? The owners of the factory, who are capitalists—who own capital. That only raises fresh questions. What is capital? What is labor? Why have some been able to accumulate vast amounts of capital, while others work for wages and own no capital? The capitalists own the factory, with its machinery and equipment, the raw materials and the power source involved, etc. But do they thus become sole owners of the iron and steel produced in the factory by our workers and thousands of their comrades? Questions multiply, and we must take them one at a time.

First, have our workers anything in common with the factory they work in? The factory contains all that is needed to produce iron and steel: suitable buildings, appropriate equipment, reserves of energy, stocks of raw materials, and auxiliary supplies. All this is necessary, but insufficient: if the workers all went on vacation at the same time, the factory would grind to a halt. Only the workers

—the labor force—can make the factory function. It is also clear, however, that without the factory and equipment the workers could not produce a single pound of iron. Thus workers on the one hand, and factory machines and raw materials on the other, have it in common to be indispensable to a particular end product. This is why they are called the *productive forces*. One can say that the productive forces encompass the whole range of means available to human beings for mastering nature and producing material goods to satisfy their needs.

The productive forces are composed of three elements:

1.   *The means of production*, generally considered to comprise on the one hand useful materials from natural sources: minerals, coal, petroleum, wood, water, etc.; and on the other hand the instruments of production: tools, machinery, and increasingly advanced equipment which makes it possible to extract or harvest useful natural materials, and then to transport and industrially transform them. In our original example these means of production are the steel mill itself with all its contents, reserves of energy, raw materials and various ingredients in stock, its machines and equipment, production lines, etc.

2.   *The labor power* of humanity itself, without which natural resources could not be extracted from above or below the ground and brought to the place where they are to be used, nor could the machines or equipment of any factory transform these natural resources into items for human use.

3.   Finally, these productive forces also include what is sometimes called indirect, or *general, labor*, which covers the skill and experience acquired by the workers over generations, the cumulative contributions of scientific and technical innovation, and the modern organization of collective labor. These latter factors have the effect of increasing the combined efficiency of machinery and equipment on the one hand, and of the workers' labor on the other. Relatively modest in the past, scientific and technical progress is now much more rapid, constituting a genuine revolution in techniques of production.

Having given this summary definition of the productive

forces, we must inquire into the relations between the workers—who hold only their own labor power—and the capitalists—who own factories with equipment and machinery and, moreover, possess liquid capital to purchase raw materials and pay workers. These differing relations to the productive forces for the purpose of producing material goods are known as *relations of production.*

But first it is necessary to point out that the productive forces, on the one hand, and the relations of production, on the other, together determine the *mode of production.* In common parlance, the terms *capitalist regime,* or the *capitalist system,* are used to describe, even if rather vaguely and generally, what is meant by "the capitalist mode of production." A mode of production is defined both by the level attained by its productive forces, and by the type of relations of production in operation. There is, moreover, a direct relationship between the *productive forces* and the *relations of production.* For example, in the Middle Ages the productive forces, especially the means of production, were as yet insufficiently developed for anything but individual peasant or artisan production. In that situation, the relations of production could, in the main, only be personal relations: between lord and serf, journeyman and master. Together, these productive forces and relations of production determined the mode of production we call feudal.

The capitalist mode of production only began to emerge when individuals who had accumulated the first capital created workshops, that is, enterprises where workers labored side by side for a wage and on their employer's account. These workers had formerly been independent masters of the product of their labor. Although the tools and methods of production had not yet changed, this form of organization of labor contained the embryo of the capitalist mode of production as we know it today. It "took off" only when mechanization—the outcome of science and technology—had transformed workshops into factories and given birth to large-scale industry.

The two characteristics of the capitalist mode of production are a high development of the productive forces and a situation in which the means of production are owned by a very small number of capitalists. At the same time, productive labor, without which these means of production could not operate, is organized so as to group millions of workers into ever more gigantic enterprises. This engenders relations of production (to which we must return) which oblige these proletarians, owning nothing but their labor, to sell it to the capitalist owners of the means of production in order to live. Thus we discover the existence of two *social classes* with objectively antagonistic interests: on the one hand, a numerically small class owning almost all the means of production and, on the other, a numerically enormous class which alone has the power to operate the means of production owned by the capitalist class. On one side, the working class, without which no production would be possible, strives to acquire the maximum share of the fruits of its labor. On the other side, the capitalist class, which owns the means of production without which nothing could be produced, also claims the maximum profits from its property. Relations of production are no longer relations between individuals, but social relations between two classes linked to each other by an insurmountable contradiction. In present-day capitalist society, production is increasingly collective or "social." There are two reasons for this: first, the system calls for an ever increasing number of proletarian producers who are not simply individual workers, side-by-side in a given enterprise, but who have been made into a real "collective" worker by the division and organization of labor; and, second, the objects produced are destined for society as a whole. Paradoxically, it is not the producers or society as a whole who direct, control, and plan this typically social production, but the small number of private owners of the means of production—who also appropriate the profit. Since production is social, equity and good sense would require it to be controlled and planned collectively for the benefit of society, and not by a minority of capitalists in their exclusive interest.

The contradiction between the private ownership of the means of production and the social nature of production is the *fundamental contradiction of the capitalist system.* This contradiction does not attenuate or soften as the capitalist system which gave rise to it develops. On the contrary, it sharpens and deepens. The more powerful capitalists come to monopolize the economic system and the state, and these, in particular, are continuously declining in numbers (as we shall see). At the same time, there is constant growth of the army of producers and of the body of nonproductive workers whose interests and aspirations are becoming more and more identified with those of the working class. There is no possible resolution of this contradiction within the framework of the capitalist mode of production, since the contradiction is of its very essence. Thus, the *class struggle* between the proletariat and its allies on the one side, and the capitalists and their upholders on the other, is not a political choice, as reactionaries make it out to be, but an objective, unavoidable necessity growing out of the very nature of capitalism.

While playing a part in determining a particular mode of production, the productive forces are also continuously progressing and changing. From the dawn of humanity people have been discovering and inventing (the wheel, harness, cart, winch, and more recently the steam engine, electricity, and atomic energy). These inventions and discoveries become new instruments of production and, by developing human skill and knowledge, make possible new and more advanced discoveries and inventions. This upward trend is continuous and infinite.

At the same time, relations of production are immobilized for long periods because they are sanctioned by laws and institutions. Economically and politically powerful persons who profit by existing relations of production try to stabilize them by giving them the force of law (e.g., guaranteeing the right to private property by law or constitution). It follows that relations of production can only be changed by violent means, by social revolution aimed at the overthrow of the "established order."

The productive forces advance constantly while, on the contrary, the relations of production remain static. The time comes when these relations of production are no longer appropriate to the level reached by the expanding forces of production, and come into conflict with them—just as a child's garment becomes too small and splits at every seam as the child grows. With productive forces at their present level, it would be possible to satisfy a host of material and cultural, individual and social needs, both conscious and latent. Many or most of these needs capitalist productive relations can but ignore, because they are geared only to the generation of profit for the capitalist class. History has never seen a privileged minority class sacrifice itself on the altar of human progress, and so the objective conflict between the development of the productive forces and the relations of production is expressed on the human level as a conflict of classes: the ruling class clinging desperately to outworn relations of production serving their class interests (a position basically *reactionary*); and the oppressed and exploited classes pressing for the radical transformation of the relations of production for the benefit of society as a whole (a position basically progressive and *revolutionary*).

3
From Subsistence to Commodities:
What Is Value?

Let us look at a given quantity of any one of the great variety of goods useful to humanity—a loaf of bread, for example. In the past such a loaf of bread would have been produced by peasants for their families from their own grain harvest. Today our loaf of bread is produced for sale by a local baker or a bread factory. In each case the bread has what is called *use value*, which is to say that it is a material object with properties suitable for the satisfaction of a human need. In general, humankind produces only material objects to satisfy physical needs (bread, clothing), cultural needs (books, paintings), or those of leisure and pleasure (games, parks).

In our first example—the peasant loaf—the use value of the object produced was solely for the producer. Today, however, the bread is *not* for the use of the producer; its use value is offered to others on the basis of exchange mediated by money. Thus, bread keeps its use value of providing so many calories for the consumer, but acquires a new value called *exchange value* because it can be exchanged for other similarly useful products. If I learn from the market that the product of the sale of a given weight of bread enables the baker to obtain a hundred sheets of writing paper, this means that a given weight of bread is *worth* a given quantity of writing paper. Exchange value is a quantitative relationship (one loaf for one hundred sheets) through which different use values (bread and paper) are exchanged. This is, of course, expressed through prices, the monetary measure of exchange value. If, for instance, the monetary value of a loaf of bread is expressed as two units of money, it is obvious that a loaf of this weight could be exchanged against all sorts of products whose exchange value is also expressed by two units of money: two lettuces, two ballpoint pens, three pairs of shoelaces, etc. When it is exchanged, the loaf of bread remains a loaf of bread and keeps all its specific qualities, but by the very fact of the exchange it becomes a commodity.

According to Marx, all commodities have the dual aspect of use value and exchange value. A commodity is a material good which has been produced in order to be introduced into the flow of trade. This means that in the present day almost all human products are commodities, since subsistence production has almost disappeared. According to their purpose, commodities can be *consumer goods* when they can be consumed as they are (food, clothes) or they can be *capital goods* when they are used to produce other objects (machines, productive equipment, raw materials, and semiprocessed goods).

Commodities came to have this universal character through a long historical process. The tools of early times were improved and diversified over the centuries, requiring ever increasing skill from their handlers until the time came when no one could operate them successfully singlehanded. This was one of a number of circumstances favorable to the specialization of workers. In the artisan stage there was already a very typical division of labor: there were artisan smiths, joiners, leather workers, etc., conducting small commodity enterprises.

These artisans were specialist independent workers who owned their own means of production, though producing for the market. So commodities were on the scene, but still in competition with subsistence production. Capital had not yet penetrated production, which was individual or familial. Whatever technical progress might have been made, workshops could not have come into being if certain people had not succeeded in accumulating large quantities of money—that is, capital—sufficient to construct and equip buildings, to buy quantities of tools and raw materials, and to pay the wages of what would henceforth be a labor force largely composed of former independent artisans.

How did a few privileged persons achieve this *primitive accumulation of capital* without which capitalism could neither begin nor develop? Briefly, it began when feudal lords and church authorities violently appropriated land which was at that time the main means of production. Louis Adolpho Thiers, the statesman and historian who was to be the destroyer of the Paris Commune of 1871, put forward relativist views of the origin of private property which Marx rebutted in the following terms in *Capital*: "In actual history it is notorious that conquest, enslavement, robbery, murder, briefly force, play the great part."[1]

In the course of time, small-scale commodity production opened a new field of operation to trade—which already encompassed grain and other agricultural products. The growth of trade enabled certain city dwellers to specialize in the purchase and resale of commodities, and thus to accumulate some commercial capital, which was then increased by the practice of usury. Small traders grew big, trade reached international proportions, arms dealers and the earliest bankers came into being.

Finally, the development of navigation and the discovery of America gave a great boost to enterprises directed at the most distant corners of the earth. Great merchants sought there spices, silks, precious stones and metals—again partly by rapine and brute force.

Spoliation of the land and appropriation of its products, international trade and the pillage of distant lands—these were the sources of most of the accumulated capital for the new process of production in the earliest workshops. Industrial capital was coming into being; capitalists strove to develop and reproduce it to generate the capitalist system and to establish firmly the ever increasing predominance of the commodity market.

From primitive accumulation to industrial capital is

really a very extensive historical process, in the course of which the worker-producers were despoiled of the tools of their trade and the product of their labor, both of which had earlier belonged to them. Total separation of the producer from the means of production is the hallmark of capitalism: the means of production are appropriated by a new class—the bourgeois—and the workers who have lost their means of production must line up at the doors of the workshops, and later the factories, to sell the only thing left to them—their labor.

Commodities, as we have seen, have both a use value and an exchange value. What gives them their use value and determines their exchange value?

Let us first consider untreated natural raw materials: for example, a vein of metal buried deep under the earth, or a great oak growing freely in the heart of a forest. We know that the metal or the oak's wood can be useful to humanity. But as long as they remain underground or in the depths of the forest, they are useless. It requires human labor for them to become useful. The ore containing the metal must be extracted, the oak must be cut down and sawed up, and both products transported to where they can be used. Multiply these examples, and it can be seen that "natural wealth" is only of *potential* value until human labor has come in to give such resources reality—that is, to make them fit for human use, in effect to give them *value*.

Take iron ore: after it reaches a mill it can only be transformed into ingots of iron and steel, laminated or cast, by the application of human labor. Some "semiprocessed" or intermediate products will leave one factory only to enter another, where the intellectual and technical work of a small number of engineers, and the manual labor of a large number of workers, will transform it into industrial machinery and equipment. A different lot of these products will go to other factories to be transformed into consumer goods. All along the line, one finds labor. The effectiveness of the workers' labor is increased by capital equipment, but even this is only *earlier* human labor incorporated or materialized. Every factory is a mass of such labor. In brief, all human products are manufactured, and are the product of human labor—labor is the only source of their value.

We have seen that commodities are goods exchanged one for another in fixed ratios, which thus have an *exchange value*. How are the exchange ratios between certain goods determined? To put it more concretely, why can a given weight of iron from one factory be exchanged for (let us suppose) one safety garment for foundry workers? This safety garment and a given weight of iron have nothing in common physically. They cannot be compared by their component elements, nor by weight or volume. Since we have to admit that the value of the one is equal to that of the other, we must conclude that the value of a protective garment and that of a given weight of metal can only be measured by an invisible common factor. This factor is labor: *the only common content of all commodities is the labor which has produced them.*

When the system of exchange began, if a smith had forged a sickle and wanted some grain for food, he would approach the peasant farmer. The smith's work and that of the peasant were at that stage *simple labor*, and for each represented "the expenditure of simple labor power which, on an average, apart from any special development, exists in the organism of every ordinary individual."[2]

The peasant could just as easily have done the smith's work, and vice versa; and, naturally, in exchanging a sickle for so much grain the peasant and the smith were exchanging as many hours of simple labor as the latter had spent producing a sickle against that quantity of grain which represented an equivalent amount of simple labor. This was not difficult to estimate.

Everyone knows that labor nowadays is not simple but *complex*. The ordinary iron and steel coming from our factories incorporates unskilled labor from the manual workers, and increasingly skilled labor from the crafts workers, the engineers, etc. This labor at different levels of skill has different values—that is to say, an equal number of hours adds more or less value to the product. On the other hand, the skilled work of artisans is partly derived from the labor of the "master artisans" who trained them. Their labor is a composite, which embodies some earlier work done by others.

Is there a common measure for simple and complex or skilled labor? Yes, for complex labor is never more than a multiple of simple labor. Suppose that one hour of complex labor in a modern factory produces an article which would have required five hours' labor from an artisan of earlier times. This means simply that complex labor is five times as productive as simple labor, that it is, in fact, simple labor multiplied.

Modern labor is complex. It is also (as we have seen), social: that is, collective labor—hundreds, even thousands of workers labor together in a single factory. The product of a factory is the fruit of the labor expended between the four walls of that factory, or immediate labor, but it is also the product of *earlier* labor embodied in the machines and equipment of the factory and in the relevant raw materials, etc. It also embodies part of what is called "general labor," or the scientific labor past and present which has contributed to all the relevant inventions and discoveries which represent society's victories in the struggle to comprehend and harness the forces of nature. Human labor embodied in a commodity is "part and parcel of the total sum of labor expended by society."[3] One may conclude that *the value of a commodity is determined by the amount of labor socially necessary to produce it,* "socially" being taken in the widest sense to mean "in the general conditions pertaining in a particular society."

It follows that the value of a commodity cannot be measured in practical terms. The value of a given weight of bread cannot be absolutely and independently determined. It is not possible to say that such value is contained in the bread; it can only be expressed in relation to that of one or more other commodities. To return to our original example, when a loaf of bread is exchanged for a hundred sheets of paper, bread expresses the value of the paper and vice versa; value can only be formulated through a relationship of equivalence. Such a relationship is, moreover, multiple; for bread could be exchanged for a thousand other commodities in a different quantity for each. For the almost unlimited number of commodities in the market to be exchanged simply and quickly, it was necessary to find a single commodity which would serve as a universal intermediary, playing the role of *general equivalent* for all other commodities. Gold and silver quickly came to the fore as general equivalents, not because of any mysterious or supernatural properties, but because, while being commodities like any other, they possess certain essential physical qualities to a greater degree: they do not deteriorate, they have low weight and volume in proportion to value, and they are easy to identify and subdivide. The early appearance of gold and silver ingots was gradually followed by that of coins struck by various states which guaranteed their weight and metal content: they became money. Later, silver and gold money was replaced by other forms: bank notes, checks, bills, etc., which we will discuss later. Once precious metals had become a general equivalent, the value of goods was expressed by a given weight of gold or silver, and then by a certain number of units of money. Instead of saying that our loaf of bread is worth a hundred sheets of paper, we say that each loaf is worth, say, two units of money. Thus, *price* is the monetary expression of the value of a commodity.

Value — amt of resources used
— amt of labor used

4
Labor Power:
A Unique Commodity
that Creates Surplus Value

Before the advent of capitalism, the peasant and the artisan would go to the market and get money in exchange for commodities which were the product of their labor. With the proceeds they then acquired various articles needed for their personal consumption. For example, the peasant might sell vegetables and buy cloth with the proceeds. The artisan weaver would do the opposite: this was called *small-scale commodity production.*

Both peasant and artisan were *selling in order to buy* and the movement of the exchange could be expressed as follows:

Commodity (C) → Money (M) → Commodity (C)

The value of (C) in the third and last stage was the same as the value of (C) in the first stage.

But soon a new actor appeared on the stage, as we have seen, a person who held money, or capital, with which to undertake exchanges as a profession. Owning only money, this person must first acquire a commodity—the weavers' cloth for example—not for personal consumption but for resale. The aim is no longer to sell in order to buy but, on the contrary, to *buy in order to sell*, or rather resell. The movement of exchange then became:

M (Money) → C (Commodity) → M'

M′ is money at the end of the transaction, and is not the same as the sum committed at the beginning of the transaction, for capitalists would never use their money for the purchase of a commodity that they could not resell for more than they had spent. Thus, M′ is greater than M: M′ equals M plus m, where "m" is what is commonly called the gain or profit, which we will refer to as *surplus value.* Moreover, the capitalist trader can only realize surplus value insofar as the artisan weaver and the rest who sell their products hand them over at less than their value: they choose to yield part of this value to the trader rather than waste much precious time chasing after customers.

It is obvious that the operation of selling to buy cannot be continuous. Weavers could not repeat it before weaving some more cloth. On the other hand, the owners of capital can always put their money back into circulation and repeat their operations as often and as quickly as possible: buying to sell, starting with money to acquire more money, which thus enables them to increase their capital. The operation is, however, limited by the fact that they cannot buy more goods than others produce since their own activities do not create new wealth. Thus, at a certain stage in their history, as we have seen, the capitalist traders realize that it is in their interests to transform themselves into capitalist manufacturers, and then industrialists, and to devote their capital to the acquisition of buildings, machinery and equipment, raw materials, and labor force—with all of which they will produce commodities for subsequent sale against money. Again, there is in the first place a certain amount of money (M); then various commodities including labor; and, at the end of the process, money again, but *more* of it: M′. The only difference is that the commodities originally purchased have been transformed into other commodities. But this does not alter the nature or the course of the operation. The movement of capital is still present, still continuous, and unlimited. Every day new amounts of raw materials, labor, etc, come into play; each day fresh quantities of commodities are produced and put on sale; money enters and leaves the enterprise daily. The formula M → C

→ M' must thus be regarded as the *general formula of capital.*

Next we must inquire into the origin of surplus value. As we saw earlier, the exchange value of a commodity is determined by the amount of social labor inherent in it, and its price is only the monetary expression of that value. Exchange cannot change the value of a commodity.

In the general formula of capital, M' becomes greater than M only because the productive forces of the factory come into play. The buildings, machines and equipment, raw materials, and labor power are purchased by the capitalist for the sum M, which is their value, but through the production process they generate a certain quantity of manufactured goods which at that point, without leaving the factory, are valued at M' = M plus m. Independently of any buying or selling operation, a new value (m) has been created simply by the entry into the production process of a commodity unlike any other and which, once purchased and put into operation, has the property of creating supplementary value or surplus value. This commodity is *labor power*, which must not be confused with work.

Marx defined labor power as "the aggregate of those mental and physical capabilities existing in a human being, which he exercises whenever he produces a use-value of any description."[4] Thus labor power is a capacity, a potential which can be left fallow or brought into action and which can be used more or less intensely. Work is the act of working ("I worked six hours yesterday"), and is also the result of bringing this faculty into action ("That's a fine piece of work").

When a worker appears at the factory gates looking for a job, what happens? Two people are involved, the worker and the capitalist (or rather a representative), who are going to make a deal: with the money in hand the capitalist buys the worker's labor power and the latter agrees to sell it. This deal is carried out exactly as if any material commodity were involved: cloth or a ballpoint pen. In other words, the capitalist buys labor power at its money value, and in exchange for this labor power agrees to pay the worker a certain wage. Just as price is the monetary expression of the value of commodities in general, the wage is the monetary expression of the value of that particular commodity represented by labor power.

We have already seen that the value of a commodity is determined by the amount of labor socially necessary to produce it. This law of value is general, and applies to labor power as much as to any other commodity. So we must ask ourselves: What makes it possible to produce labor power? What determines its value? It goes without saying that to exist and reproduce itself labor power requires the worker to be fed, clothed and sheltered from the elements, to be cared for when ill, to have transport to and from the factory, etc. In brief, the production and maintenance of labor power requires means of subsistence the value of which represents the value of this labor power. The expression "means of subsistence" must be widely interpreted. Thus the day will come when the worker will be too old to work, and will have to be replaced by his or her children. The means of subsistence have, therefore, to be applied to the worker and the worker's family.

The concrete expression of this concept of means of subsistence varies in space and time. In space it does not encompass the same amount of goods in an "underdeveloped" as in an "advanced" society. (This topic will recur when we come to discuss imperialism.) To take Europe as an example, it is obvious that the products necessary for the reconstitution of the labor force are not the same now as, say, 150 years ago. Civilization has brought in new factors, and there are more needs to be satisfied. For example, holidays with pay are now considered necessary to maintain the labor force. Thus a social factor (which varies by country and type of society) and an historic factor (varying through time in the same country) enter into the determination of labor power. But "in a given country, at a given period, the average quantity of the means of subsistence necessary for the laborer is practically known."[?]

The capitalist buys the labor power of many workers,

but this same capital must also buy the means of production to enable labor power to function. Thus the capitalist transforms money capital into productive capital which includes the following factors: (1) buildings, tools, and equipment; (2) raw materials and other supplies; (3) labor power.

By "other supplies" are meant products which do not become incorporated into the finished goods as are raw materials but which are, nevertheless, essential to their production (e.g., lubricants for the machinery, energy required to put them into action, and so on).

When applied, the workers' labor power has two effects: on the one hand, it *transfers* into the final product the value contained in the means of production used. If the means of production are completely consumed, their whole value is transferred, but if it is a matter of buildings, tools, and equipment which depreciate and last a long time, only a small part is transferred. On the other hand, all new value is the outcome of labor; this *creates* new value which is incorporated into the commodity in the process of its manufacture.

Let us suppose a worker to have been engaged at an hourly rate which will pay sixty units of currency for an eight-hour day. These sixty units represent the value of the worker's labor power, which is the value of the means of subsistence for himself or herself and the family. Let us suppose that after four hours' work the worker's labor power has created value equal to his or her daily subsistence requirements, in this case sixty units. But, as noted, during these four hours he or she has not only added new value, but also transferred to the product (1) the value of the raw materials that are incorporated (embodied) in the final product produced and (2) the value of the machinery that has been used up (worn away) during the manufacture of the product—which in this case amounts to forty units of value.

The value of the commodities produced in four hours will be: 40 + 60 = 100. At this point the capitalist has committed one hundred units of capital and acquired products that are also worth one hundred units. If that were the end of the day's work, the capitalist would make nothing and might just as well close the factory and retire to a good climate; and the capitalist system would collapse. For the system to function the worker must labor for longer than it takes to *create* a value equal to that of his or her daily requirement of the means of subsistence, known as *necessary labor time,* that is, what is necessary to reproduce his or her labor power.

For this reason the working day is fixed at eight hours rather than four, entitling the capitalist to use the worker's labor power for eight hours. During the second four-hour period the capitalist will again supply means of production by which another value of 40 units will be transferred to the final product. But the worker's extra four hours of labor will not be paid for, since his or her boss has already paid 60 units as the total value of labor power—which has been recouped during the first four hours. Thus the latter part of the day's work is supplementary, unpaid labor which is usually called *surplus labor.*

During the four hours' surplus labor the value of commodities produced will again be 40 units (derived from the value of the means of production transferred) plus 60 units (added by labor) equals 100 units. This value is the property of the capitalist, but this time he or she will have spent only 40 units to bring it into being, since the 60 units added by surplus labor are not paid for. The 60 units, the product of surplus labor, is *surplus value*—the product of capitalist exploitation. It can be measured by ascertaining the ratio between the amount of time given to surplus labor and that to necessary labor. In our example the *rate of exploitation* or the *rate of surplus value* is four over four equals 100 percent.

Of course this example is schematic and designed only to translate the analysis of reality into simple terms. But the above rate of surplus value is not unrealistic. In 1962 a French economist calculated that the general annual rate of surplus value in France was 166 percent, meaning that overall, "the wages and social payments of a productive worker would be worth three hours of an eight hour day and capital would directly appropriate the remaining five."[6] The author was correct in writing "capital" and not "the capitalist," for surplus value is far from remaining wholly in the hands of the capitalist who is its direct and immediate beneficiary.

It is now necessary to state some new definitions which we shall need as we proceed.

We have seen that there are two elements in the value of any commodity: (a) all or part of the value of the buildings, tools and equipment, raw materials, and supplies is simply transferred to the product in the course of the process of production; this part of the capital does not change and is called *constant capital*; (b) on the other hand, that portion and only that portion of capital going to wages and salaries provides an increase in value, or surplus value, and it is called *variable capital*.

As surplus value represents unpaid labor, the capitalist will naturally seek to maximize its growth. The number of hours of necessary labor is practically invariable at any given time, since it represents the average value of the means of subsistence necessary to maintain labor power. But if the capitalist can increase the hours in a working day without raising wages, this will increase the hours producing surplus labor and so increase surplus value. *Absolute surplus value* is used to describe surplus value obtained solely by lengthening the working day. The issue of the length of the working day was at the heart of the great workers' struggles of the nineteenth century. First the bosses lengthened it to fourteen hours and more; then the class struggle developed and made it possible to reduce the working day to twelve hours, then ten, and finally eight hours.

How can capitalists increase surplus value even when the length of the working day remains stable over a long period, as is generally the case today? For they are always striving to obtain such an increase. They can achieve it by decreasing the time required for necessary labor, that is, by creating conditions to modify the internal relationship within a fixed eight-hour day—between the time spent in necessary labor and that in surplus labor. An increase in surplus value brought about by modifying this internal relationship is called *relative surplus value.*

Thus a reduction in necessary labor time is most likely to be brought about if scientific and technical advances increase productivity in the manufacture of subsistence goods required to maintain labor power: food, clothes, etc. A reduction in the value of such goods leads to a parallel reduction in the value of labor power and so in necessary labor time. For example, necessary labor time might decrease from four to three hours in an eight-hour day and surplus labor increase correspondingly from four to five hours, with a relative increase in surplus value. Capitalists understand very well that increased productivity of labor without proportionate wage increases constitutes a reinforcement of the exploitation of labor, and they have made great use of this approach since the Second World War.

It is equally well understood that exploitation can be reinforced not only by increasing the *productivity of labor* (increased results with unchanged effort), but also by increasing the *intensity of labor* by requiring of the worker greater physical effort: speeding up, overseeing more machinery, etc. In this case the surplus labor time remains the same, but its product is increased by greater effort. The effect is the same as that of lengthening the working day without raising wages; the worker puts as much productive effort into eight hours as would normally be put into ten. There is a subsequent increase in absolute surplus value.

Without surplus value the capitalists could not have come into being, nor could they survive, so that it is always in their interests to seek to increase it either by playing on relative or absolute surplus value, or by some combination of the two. Surplus value lies at the root of the capitalist mode of production and can be created only by the surplus labor of the proletarians for which they are not paid. This gives rise to an antagonism between the working class and capitalist class which cannot be resolved in the framework of the system, since it flows from its controlling laws. That is to say, among other things, that there cannot be good capitalists, only more or less bad ones, since it is in the nature of the capitalist to appropriate surplus value extorted from the proletarian.

5
Early Conclusions

Before pursuing further our study of the capitalist mode of production itself, we should now step aside and try to bring together, from what we have seen so far, some general principles and early deductions which will illuminate subsequent materials. We have already made enough observations to provide concrete examples for our reflection.

We have already observed that in the world, that is, in nature and in society, *all is movement*, change, constant transformation. Slavery gave rise to feudalism and feudal society in its turn gave rise to capitalism. The productive forces develop at varying rates, but never stand still. Though capitalism does not change its essential character, it is constantly varying its manifestations, affected, for example, by scientific and technological progress or working-class resistance. We are now in the historic epoch when the major problem of the day is that of capitalism's total replacement by a different mode of production and a new society: socialism.

What practical conclusions can we draw? We must realize that in the way we look at everything we must always try to embrace this movement, to perceive what is declining at any given moment, and may be about to vanish and what, on the contrary, is developing and may be about to come into being. That which is on the verge of disappearing may yet seem all-powerful and that which is developing may seem minor or even invisible on casual inspection. It is, however, that which is coming to birth or growing that is important, and not that which is in decay and nearing its end.

If we probe a little more deeply we see that the world—or a society—is a whole whose various parts condition each other reciprocally. No phenomenon we can observe is isolated, independent of any other. On the contrary, all are linked together and *act upon each other*. Thus we saw in the previous chapter that the progress of science and technology gives rises to greater productivity, which in turn is one of the principle means by which capitalists increase their surplus value. Yet at first sight what could be further from each other than scientific progress and surplus value? Moreover, while scientific progress and its technical application have had an impact on surplus value which might not have been foreseen, as soon as this impact became apparent a reverse effect developed to increase scientific research, especially in fields likely to lead to technical innovations which would produce higher relative surplus value.

This way of looking at phenomena, in motion and in transformation, in their connections and reciprocal effects, is known as the *dialectic* or the dialectical method. It is the only way in which we can analyze the nature and dynamics of the society in which we live.

There is still more to the dialectic. The pattern of constant change and movement in nature and society is neither regular nor mechanical. If water is set on a high flame its temperature rises rapidly from 20° (C) to 99°. There has been a considerable *quantitative change* in water temperature, but at 99° the water is still water—that is, a liquid. However, if the process continues to 100°, water will turn into steam—a sudden change of state. At this point a *qualitative change* takes place as a consequence of the earlier quantitative change.

Similarly, the primitive accumulation of capital discussed earlier was not the work of a single day. Over a great many years capital accumulated in the possession of a few, progressing through major quantitative changes, yet for a long time not generating a new mode of production. Capital existed, but capitalism was not yet in being. Only when accumulation reached a certain quantitative level could new capital be invested, not in the old manner (land rents, usury, or trade) but rather in the large-scale acquisition of the instruments of production. Capital took to manufacture and became industrial. Feudalism gave way to the capitalist mode of production, bringing radical qualititative changes in the very nature of societies.

In that case, transition to the qualitatively new was gradual. But there are instances where qualitative change occurs very rapidly: the bourgeois political revolution in France in 1789, the October 1917 socialist revolution in Russia, etc. One can then say that change proceeds "by leaps." These leaps, however, always follow continuous, progressive accumulation of quantitative changes. Transition from quantitative to qualitative change is one of the principles of the dialectic which, like all others, has been discovered by close study of the real world.

Another, perhaps the most fundamental, principle of the dialectic is the presence of *contradictions* at all times and in all places, in the world and in society. For instance, we have already noticed the contradiction between the present level of development of the productive forces and capitalist productive relations, and another contradiction between capital and labor or rather, between the capitalist class or bourgeoisie and the working class or proletariat. We shall come across many other contradictions, but from now on we should take into account the proposition that contradiction is universal. How can we define contradiction? In the first place, it is inherent in the very nature of things. Let us return to boiling water. Scientists explain that there are *internal* and contradictory forces of cohesion and dispersion in the molecules of water. These forces exist unobserved when the temperature of the water lies between 0°(C) and 100°. When the temperature is raised above 100°, due to an *external* phenomenon, the nature of water is not changed, but the equilibrium is broken between the internal forces of dispersion and those of cohesion, and thus water changes its state.

Similarly, the contradiction between bourgeoisie and proletariat is of the very essence of the capitalist mode of production. If it did not exist, neither would the capitalist mode of production. Thus there is a necessary *unity* between the two elements of the contradiction which cannot exist without the other: in a capitalist society one cannot conceive of the proletariat without the bourgeoisie and vice versa. It is the fundamental struggle between these contradictory elements which gives rise to their unity and defines the contradiction itself. Moreover, the struggle between opposites does not take place in a vacuum. In society, as in nature, external events can favor one or the other of the opposites. External causes (technical progress, class alliances, etc.) affect the contradiction between the bourgeoisie and the proletariat so that sometimes the bourgeoisie is entirely on top and sometimes the proletariat makes gains. The conflict between the two elements of the contradiction is always present, but the relation of forces between them is in constant motion. It is therefore of great importance to determine which is the *principal element* of the contradiction at any particular time.

Let us also note that, as seems obvious, every phenomenon has its own contradictions, which cannot be identified with those of any other phenomenon. It follows that identical solutions cannot be applied to different contradictions. Each specific contradiction requires a profound analysis leading to action particular to its nature.

Finally, in every society there will be an infinite number of different contradictions of varying levels of significance. It is, therefore, necessary to distinguish the principal contradiction from secondary contradictions. Later we shall see that contradictions arise within the bourgeoisie and, sometimes, within the proletariat — or between the proletariat and its allies. On analysis, however, these contradictions appear to be secondary in relation to the principal contradiction between the bourgeoisie and its allies on the one hand, and the proletariat and its allies on the other. There can be no strategy for the class struggle until the respective importance of the various contradictions has been established for a particular time, since this can vary with the perpetual movement of society.

Earlier discussions were focused on material conditions of production and exchange—the economic basis of society. Early on, however, attention also inevitably turned to the capitalists who have appropriated the state, and we noticed that the class which profits from capitalist productive relations, the bourgeoisie, has been at pains to institutionalize these relations by embodying them in legal codes and enactments. The state, the law and its codifications, are abstract ideas and not of an economic nature, yet we must look at them more closely.

Clearly humankind's first need is to maintain physical life; production of the means of subsistence (clothing, food, housing) and the conditions under which they are produced are of immediate, fundamental, and permanent importance. This is why the mode of production, the productive forces, and the social relations of production which determine them are regarded in the Marxist analysis as being the *basic economic infrastructure* of society. A society can only be built upon such an economic infrastructure, as a house on its foundations.

Society, however, is not composed simply of its infrastructure. Humankind has the faculties of thought and conscience and, living in society, finds social rules and institutions essential. Everything that is built up on the economic infrastructure—the state and its instruments and institutions of all kinds, opinions and beliefs, morality and culture—all can be grouped together as what is called the *superstructure.*

From the foregoing, and using the analogy between society and a house, it follows that the superstructure is determined by the infrastructure: on particular foundations only one type of house can be built and no other. The superstructure is generally described as the *reflec-*

tion of the economic infrastructure in the political and juridical institutions and in the customs and consciousness of humankind. The ideas dominant in contemporary Western societies, for example, were derived from established productive relations: the *existence* of private property has created the idea of the *right* to property and enshrined it in law and custom; it is imposed and guaranteed by the state; social inequality is justified by respected philosophies, etc.

As a reflection of the infrastructure, superstructure is, therefore, not a fixed dimension. When the material base of a society is subjected to changes and disturbances, this will sooner or later affect the superstructure, which will tend to adapt to changed material conditions. However, the dialectic has taught us that the relations between phenomena are never mechanical or one-directional and that the effect of "a" on "b" is always followed by the reaction of "b" on "a." To put it another way, although the superstructure originates as a reflection of the infrastructure which determined it, yet it has a life of its own and becomes an active force which may, in its turn, influence the economic structure of society. It has in fact been observed that the superstructure is usually more resistant to change than the infrastructure which gave rise to it. We now know by experience that when the productive relations of a country have been transformed from capitalism to socialism—at least in their fundamentals—the old ideological superstructure persists for many long years in thought and consciousness and obstructs the construction of the new society.

Yet we are still considering a concept of the world and of history in which both the social organization of human communities and the ideas and opinions accepted within them are determined by the material conditions of life and the economic system within which the means of subsistence are produced. Ideas and beliefs are neither absolute nor eternal; they obey the laws of movement and change, and of the reciprocity of relations between phenomena. This concept derives from observation and scientific analy-

sis and is called *historical materialism* because it attrib-
utes a primary role to the material base.

We have made several references to class antagonisms
and have defined the bourgeois or capitalist class as that
which owns the means of production and the proletariat
as the class deprived in the process of production of any
alternative but selling its labor power to the bourgeoisie.
From this it appears that a *social class* is a grouping of
people defined by its position and function in the system
of social production.

In history it has always been thus: in every society
where the means of production are private property there
are two complementary classes constituting the fundamental basis of that society. In antiquity there were pa-
trician owners of the land and the slaves who worked it, in
the Middle Ages the class of feudal lords and the class
of serfs. The two principal classes are always by nature
antagonistic.

It follows that even though they may be quite numerous, other social groups such as teachers, or the army, are
not classes in the context of historical materialism because they cannot be defined by reference to the productive
relations which are the basis of social organization. There
are, however, groups of persons in capitalist society who
are neither bourgeois nor proletarian and yet play a specific part in the system of social production: the peasan-
try, small traders, artisans, etc. These groups are social
classes but, in a sense, secondary or intermediate classes
because, on the one hand, they are less clearly defined
in relation to the dominant productive relations than are
the bourgeoisie and the proletariat and, on the other
hand, their fate effectively will be determined by the
development of relations between the two principal classes.
It will be possible to make a deeper study of their case
only when we have elaborated our basic study of the capitalist mode of production.

A social class such as the proletariat is thus primarily
an objective reality which is the historical outcome of the
interplay of productive relations. A social class is also,

however, a subjective reality based on the consciousness every member acquires of being a unit of the class as a whole and of being able to define him or herself only within its context. For instance, the common experience of exploitation is the subjective condition for the appearance of proletarian solidarity, but this can only reach its full development when every proletarian deliberately wills it and recognizes solidarity as a weapon. That is a rough definition of *class consciousness.*

How does class consciousness arise and grow within the working class? During daily labor class consciousness stirs as workers conceptualize the exploitation experienced in common with their companions, and as they begin to analyze the system which gives rise to it. But class consciousness develops most clearly when the permanent antagonism between exploiter and exploited is reflected in concrete acts and, more especially, when it leads to sharp confrontations—that is, to *class struggle* and open conflicts between proletarians and capitalists in the factory or workers and the bourgeois state outside it. When the workers become fully aware of the nature of the capitalist mode of production and of capitalist society as a whole, the class struggle becomes infinitely more effective. When this awareness permeates the mass of the working class it becomes *the ideology of the proletariat,* that is, a total, coherent conception of society and its possibilities for the future. This ideology of the proletariat is, on the one hand, the product of class struggle and, on the other, relies on that same class struggle as the only means of resolving the contradiction between bourgeoisie and proletariat. We are brought back to the dialectic.

Thus class struggle is at the same time a collective confrontation with a concrete purpose and the development of consciousness for the benefit of the community in struggle. It is in every way conducive to progress. It is class struggle and the victories of exploited and subordinated classes which alone made it possible to overcome the contradictions between antagonistic classes in the past. And it can do so again in the future, giving rise to a new and better society: *class struggle is the engine of history.*

6
Profit:
The Rolling Stone
that Gathers Moss

We have seen that surplus value is created only in the context of the production of material goods for the purpose of exchange, that is, commodities: without such production there is no surplus value.

We strove to uncover the real, basic nature of surplus value: unpaid surplus labor. This real nature is usually hidden. If a worker did not ferret it out he or she might toil at bench or machine for another twenty years without surplus value becoming manifest and obvious. On the other hand, it is clear and even obvious that the capitalist factory owner makes a *profit* which is only the visible, monetary form of surplus value. To throw light on it we need to devote some time and attention to the process of *circulation of capital.*

We have already seen that the formula M→C→M′ is the general formula of capital. This capital first takes a monetary form (M), then the capitalist turns money into a commodity-means of production in order to manufacture commodities for sale (all this is represented by C). And, finally, the sale of these commodities transforms them in their turn into money (M′). This circulating movement of capital can be seen in the figure.

In the inner circle money capital is seen transforming itself into productive capital (buildings, tools, raw materials, supplies, labor power); the impact of labor turning this productive capital into commodity capital; and, fi-

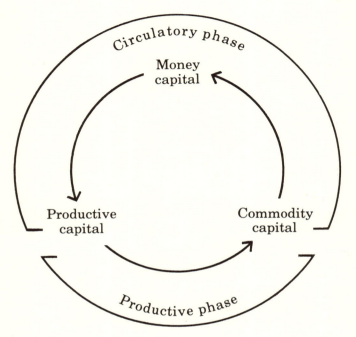

nally, the sale of the commodities turning it once more into money capital so that the circle can start again.

The outer circle shows the circulatory movement divided into two different phases:

1.   *A phase of production* (transformation of productive capital into commodity capital), taking place entirely within the factory;

2.   *A phase of circulation* as such, taking place outside the factory in the course of which the sale of commodities produces money which is immediately reinvested in commodities to be used for new production.

The movement is continuous and less schematic than in our Figure 1. The movement from one part of the cycle to another is continuous, but it cannot depart from the prescribed path. As for the productive phase and the circulatory phase, they are inseparable and are in a dialectical relationship: if one loses speed it slows down the other, and vice versa. It is in the interests of the capitalists that the cycle be completed as rapidly as possible. Foremen pass the instructions of the bosses down the production line: the factory must run smoothly without hindrance or delay —so much for the phase of production.

With regard to the phase of circulation, the owner tries to sell the commodities immediately upon production. There is no time to lose, for the greater the speed of circulation of capital the greater will be the surplus value or profit which accrues to the capitalist in a given time, since there is in each cycle only so much surplus labor to create it. This explains the need to rely on specialists in trade and distribution for the disposal of products in an increasingly complex capitalist society. It is true that the entrepreneur has to divert part of the potential profit to these specialists, but this is more than recouped in higher profit which follows the increased speed of circulation of capital brought about by their services. We shall look at this in greater detail when we investigate trade.

Here we must make a digression. During the metamorphoses of capital (money into goods and goods into money), capitalists incur special costs, expenses not directly involved in production proper, and so not themselves productive. Even when using special commercial channels for the distribution of products, capitalists need a purchasing and sales service, they need administration and accounts departments, they must meet bank charges and the costs of conserving their means of production (maintenance of plant and buildings, insurance, the stockpiling of supplies, etc.); there are also packing and handling charges, etc. In brief, entrepreneurs must meet these costs of circulating capital, which add nothing to the value of commodities coming out of the factory but are nonetheless necessary to the realization of the value of commodities, that is, the conversion of their value into money. These costs must be charged against surplus value and deducted from profit. Since their impact on the total volume of profit is, however, not significant, we shall disregard them in our further analysis.

Finally, a word on transport costs, which are not part of the costs of circulating capital. It is not usually possible for a commodity to be consumed where it is produced. Iron ore is of no more use at the shaft head than down the mine. The use value of any product can only be realized if it is put within the user's reach. Thus transport adds to the value of the commodity and must be regarded as an extension of production.

Let us now address ourselves to the problem of the transformation of surplus value into profit, first reviewing some facts we have learned. There are three elements in the value of a commodity:

1.   A small proportion of the value of the instruments of production (buildings, tools, equipment) equivalent to their depreciation is *transferred* to the commodity.

2.   The whole value of the materials of production consumed (raw materials and supplies) is transferred to the commodity.

3.   The labor power of the labor force, on the other hand, creates *new value*, part of which (necessary labor) is paid for in wages and part of which (surplus labor) is appropriated by the capitalist and called surplus value. The value in items (1) and (2) does not change during the process of production, as it is simply transferred. The capital invested under (1) and (2) is called *fixed capital*, represented as "c."

On the other hand, the capital invested under (3), that is, in wages, is that part which varies during the process of production since it is increased by surplus value. It is called *variable capital* or "v." We shall now designate as "pl" the new value created and not paid for, that is, surplus value or the product of surplus labor. Thus if "M" is the value of a given commodity the following equation applies:

$$M = c + v + pl$$

which is merely a schematic, algebraic expression of the law of value.

Let us now consider a capitalist who has invested a total capital of 850 units (this could be in millions of francs or dollars) and let us suppose it to be divided as follows between the three elements we have just described:

1. Seven hundred and fifty units are invested in instruments of production (buildings, equipment, machines, tools, etc.). We will suppose, quite arbitrarily, that these instruments would be worn out in ten years, that is, depreciation at 10 percent per annum or seventy-five units. This capital of seventy-five represents the value transmitted to the commodities produced in one year. These figures are shown in the first line of Table 1.

2. Our capitalist decides to allocate 50 units for the purchase of materials of production (raw materials, supplies, etc.). This could be the cost of requirements for four months, and such materials would have to be replaced three times a year using the proceeds of sales of commodities from the previous cycle—that is, a transmitted value of $3 \times 50 = 150$ for the whole year. These figures are shown in the second line of the table.

3. Our capitalist also decides to allocate fifty units to payment of workers covering three months' wages. The sale of commodities produced during the first three months provides for replacement of the capital advanced, so that there will be four replacements a year, or a value transmitted to a year's production of commodities of $50 \times 4 = 200$. These figures are shown in line three of the table.

4. We must, however, also take into account the surplus value produced in a year. If we estimate that workers carry out three hours of unpaid surplus labor for every two hours of necessary labor for wages, then surplus value to wages will be in a ratio of 3:2, giving in a year the figure of 300, which we enter at the bottom of the table.

Our capitalist has invested a total of 850 units but has transmitted only part of this to one year's production of commodities. This transmitted value is $75 + 150 = 225$ of fixed capital—"c"—+ 200 of variable capital—"v"—giving a

	Total capital invested	Circulation time	Value transmitted in 1 year
1. Instruments of production	750	10 years	75
2. Materials	50	4 months	150
3. Wages	50	3 months	200
Total capital invested	850		
Cost of production of commodities produced in 1 year			425
Surplus value produced in 1 year			300
Value of 1 year's production			725

total of 425 units which the capitalist sees as the *cost of production* or prime cost of the commodities produced in a year. But the value of these commodities is greater:

$$M = 225c + 200v + 300pl = 725$$

If, as is usually the case, the capitalist has sold commodities at their value of 725 he or she will say, "I have an annual profit of 725, less my outlay or prime costs of production of 425, that is, 300": and will be correct. Profit is equal to surplus value, but surplus value is incorporated in the value of the commodities whether they be sold or not, whereas profit appears only at the moment of sale—surplus value becoming profit only when it is realized and transformed into money or capital. Our interest is centered on surplus value because it expresses the exploitation characteristic of the system, but the capitalist is concerned with the money profit which goes into his or her coffers. As Marx put it:

Surplus value and rate of surplus value are, relatively, the invisible and unknown essence that wants investigating while the rate of profit and therefore the appearance of surplus value in the form of profit are revealed on the surface of the phenomenon.[1]

It will be remembered that the *ratio of surplus value* is equal to the ratio between the value of surplus labor and that of necessary labor, that is, "pl" which, in our example, gives:

$$\frac{300pl}{200v} = 150\%$$

However, in order to calculate the *rate of profit*, how will the capitalist reckon profit? By considering the total capital "put into" the interprise, in our example 850, he or she will conclude that the rate of profit is:

$$\frac{300}{850} = 35.3\%$$

Thus the rate of profit is very different from the rate of surplus value. The latter measures the degree to which the worker is exploited and the former the return on invested capital. Yet without surplus value there would be no profit. In the above reckoning: $\frac{300}{850}$ is the surplus value. If this were absent, the ratio of $\frac{300}{850}$ would be $\frac{0}{850}$ and 0 divided by 850 equals 0. Thus if we symbolize total capital invested as "C" the rate of profit is obtained by the formula "$\frac{pl}{C}$." But we saw earlier that total capital invested falls into two parts: one of fixed capital or "c," and one of variable capital or "v," so the formula for the rate of profit is better expressed as: $\frac{pl}{c + v}$.

We have also seen that there is a direct relationship between "pl" and "v," that is, between the value or duration of surplus labor and the value or duration of necessary labor. In 1962 it was possible to calculate that in France on an average in every eight hours of work there were five hours of surplus labor and three hours of necessary labor. Of course, this ratio can and does vary, but only slowly and within limits. For convenience we will take it as fixed and so replace our earlier example with the formula $\dfrac{5}{c+3}$ for the rate of profit. This peculiar formula contains the figures 5 and 3 and the letter "c," that is, an unknown quantity representing fixed capital. Common sense and observation tell us that "c" will vary considerably from one enterprise to another. In a capital-intensive industry like those producing automobiles or airplanes, for example, the machinery and equipment is very much more valuable than in, say, a quarrying enterprise. One might take "c" to be worth 12 units in the one case and 2 in the other, which gives us the following rate of profit:

$$\frac{5}{12+3} = \frac{5}{15} = 33.3\% \text{ and } \frac{5}{2+3} = \frac{5}{5} = 100\%$$

This shows that if "v" is constant (and hence also "pl"), the rate of profit may vary considerably as a function of the value of "c"—fixed capital. Thus within the total capital of an enterprise it is important to consider the relation between that portion invested in fixed capital and that in variable capital; that is, "the payment of wages." This relationship is called the *organic composition of capital* expressed in the formula: $\dfrac{c}{v}$.

Still assuming "pl" and "v" to be constant, it would seem that the rate of profit would vary greatly as between enterprises or even more between branches of industry because of their very different organic compositions of capital. But the general impression of the lay person is quite to the contrary, and it is generally believed that the profit derived by capitalists from, say, steel mills does not differ greatly from that accruing to those in the chemical, metallurgical, or electrical industries. This idea is not erroneous: but how can this be?

First, let us recall the importance of the speed of circulation of capital or, to put this another way, the number of cycles of production that can be completed within a given time. Some industries may complete three cycles in six months and others ten or even twenty. This can often counterbalance the effect of the organic composition of capital on the rate of profit.

This relative equalization of the rate of profit, which can be empirically observed, depends, however, most of all on competition between different fields of capital investment. Let us suppose that the average rate of industrial profit is 20 percent at one particular time and arises from rates of 30 percent in one industry and 10 percent in another. This will give food for thought to capitalists receiving only 10 percent and those who have fresh capital to invest. Both will be inclined to turn away from the industries with a 10 percent rate of profit to invest their capital in those offering a return of 30 percent. Production in the first group will fall even to the point where there is a shortage of the commodities they produce; there will then be a rise in those prices and thus increased profits. The reverse will occur in the industries which were at first most favored as the capital flowing into them produces a drop in prices and profit.

Much more could be said on this subject, but that would divert us considerably from our main purpose. It is important to remember that comparisons between different industries as avenues of investment for capital brings about a general rate of profit or *average rate of profit* to which various separate rates of profit constantly tend to approximate. Rates of profit are never exactly the same throughout an economy, but the tendency for them to equalize is an observed feature of capitalism in conditions of free competition.

It must be added that in any particular country the sum of capitalist profit can only be the same as that of the national total of surplus value appropriated, since all profit is no more than surplus value realized in money. It follows that capitalists whose rate of profit is above the average are really appropriating more than their share of national surplus value. Similarly, capitalists whose rate of profit is below the average are actually appropriating less than their share of national surplus value. The one group can gain only at the expense of the other. We shall find this observation very useful when we look at monopoly capitalism as it is today and the contradictions it engenders within the capitalist class as a whole.

7
Profit in Various Guises:
Industrial, Commercial, Interest,
and Bank Rates

Up to now we have thought of profit only in its industrial form. This was justified by the fact that industrial profit is the greatest in volume and because it plays a fundamental role, since industrial capital is the only sector in which the appropriation of surplus value occurs. But capital and profit take other forms, the most important of which are *commercial capital* and *commercial profit*, which are constantly on the increase.

Earlier on we stressed the importance for capitalists of the speed of circulation of capital, and noted that capitalists usually try to accelerate this circulation by entrusting the disposal of their products to specialists in commerce and distribution and by feeding part of their profits to these specialists in remuneration for their services.

This can easily be understood by turning to the formula and definition of annual circulation of profit which is equal to: $\dfrac{pl}{C}$, when "C" represents *total* capital invested, composed of constant capital ("c") and variable capital ("v"), the latter devoted to meeting the wage bill. Hence the rate of profit: $\dfrac{pl}{c + v}$.

In this context let us compare two different but equal capital sums, C′ and C″, assuming that they carry the

49

same rate of surplus value, say, 100 percent, and have the same organic composition. For example:

$$C' = C'' = 80c + 20v = 100.$$

C', however, circulates twice in one year and C" only once; thus in a single year C' will have produced surplus value equal to twice 20v or 40pl while C" will have produced surplus value equal to only once 20v or 20pl. The rate of profit of capital C' will be: $\frac{40}{100}$ = 40% and that of C": $\frac{20}{100}$ = 20%. All else being equal, the rate of profit will be twice as high if the speed of circulation of capital is twice as fast. Not only does a faster rate of circulation of capital make it possible to realize surplus value more rapidly, but it also increases its absolute value within a given time.

If industrial capitalists try to distribute their own products and sell them to consumers they will encounter all sorts of difficulties that will take up a lot of time and financial resources; they will soon decide that it is no use trying to be jacks of all trades. Experience shows them that selling to entrepreneurs with multiple outlets and good financial backing or to specialists in large-scale mail order distribution enables their competitors to "get their money back" more quickly, thereby greatly increasing their profits. The capitalists realize that the considerable benefit to be gained from more rapid circulation of capital can be enjoyed while conceding only a reasonable share to the commercial sector. This applies especially to all consumer goods industries and to a lesser extent to capital goods industries, which are in any case less numerous.

Thus, in advanced capitalist economies a vast commercial sector has been established and developed, with a tendency to spread its tentacles throughout the economy. How are we to analyze this commercial capital?

The commercial capitalist is a specialist who buys all or part of the industrial capitalists' production at an agreed price and resells these commodities at a higher price, although they have not been transformed in any way. This

means that at the price agreed upon between the industrialist and the middleman the commodity realizes only
part of the surplus value contained in it. This is the part
appropriated by the industrial capitalist. The other part is
left to the middleman as payment for his or her services
and is realized only when the commodity is finally sold to
the consumer. The commercial capitalist believes that his
or her operations create new value and is not alone in be-
lieving or pretending this, since the state defines both commercial and industrial profit as "added value." This is only
an illusion; commercial profit is really a value preempted
or extracted from total value for the benefit of commercial capital. No value is created outside the productive
sector. This means that there is, in one sense, an objective conflict of interest between industrial and commercial capital, since they share a given amount of surplus
value. At the same time it is in their common interest to
maximize surplus value, which entails increasing exploitation of labor. Within the capitalist class there is a contradiction between industrial and commercial capital, but
this is secondary to the *principal* contradiction between
the capitalist class as a whole and the proletariat.

Moreover, in practice the secondary contradiction between industrial and commercial capital is in general resolved by the fact that the rate of commercial profit cannot for long diverge far from the average rate of profit
previously defined. If the rate of commercial profit were
actually to rise much above the industrial rate, it would
then be to the interest of industrial capitalists to invest
in the commercial sector and distribute their own products
to the consumers. Competition between forms of capitalist
investment operates not only within each sector, but between the various sectors. The resulting average rate of
profit is a trend applicable to the economy as a whole.

Industrial and commercial capitalists rarely operate
solely on their own capital; they borrow money on which
they pay *interest*. Major companies issue *shares*, that is,
IOUs, issued to many savers, large or small, in exchange
for an interest-bearing loan. A saver with 3,000 units of

money can subscribe to 30 shares of 100 units in a particular company, which undertakes to return the 3,000 units in 15 or 20 years and to pay 7 or 8 percent annual interest for the duration of the loan. The industrial giants also often receive loans (many of them at low interest) from the state. Banks often give medium-term loans to companies which are their customers, and discount the bills of exchange or drafts which they receive; that is, they advance to their clients sums equivalent to these bills of exchange for the period until the bills fall due (usually three to six months) and charge a discount or interest for this service. What we have described are different forms of interest-bearing money loans (long-, medium-, or short-term) all of which enable the capitalist who receives them to expand operations.

How can we explain the return or interest received by those who lend money? We know money does not have the inherent property of generating money. Money does not "breed." If, however, money takes the form of capital invested in a process of production, it appropriates surplus value and brings in a profit. The sum of 3,000 units of money predicated above as savings does not generate anything while hidden in a cupboard. It began to bring in an interest of 8 percent only when invested in shares, because the company in turn invested that money in a productive process which generated profit. The interest paid at the end of the year is simply part of the surplus value generated by the original sum applied as productive capital. It follows that the interest rate must be lower than the rate of profit. If the capitalist who borrows the 3,000 knows that by putting it with many other sums he or she can create a profit of 20 percent, he or she can offer 8 percent to the investor and retain a net profit of 12 percent.

Surplus value is created only in the productive process, but the industrial capitalist can allocate a share to the commercial capitalist, or another share called interest to the holder of cash which can be used to create additional surplus value (this last point is important, since share issues are on the increase). All this amounts to a shared surplus value between the interested parties. As we shall see, there are more of these interested parties than the commercial capitalist and the lender of money.

Now let us turn to those whose sole occupation is the manipulation of money: the bankers. How is it that these people in particular can realize profit at a rate equal to the average general rate of profit (otherwise there would be no bankers), although their sole function is to lend money at a rate of interest which is, by definition, lower than the average rate of profit? This paradox is, of course, illusory.

Our first inquiry relates to the source of banking capital. More precisely, what do the bankers use for their operations? At the start, they certainly invest their own capital to set up a head office, branches, customer counters, etc. Suppose that a large bank thus invests the sum of 100 units of its own capital. Across its counters it will soon attract deposits far in excess of its own capital. It is not unrealistic to postulate that these deposits will soon reach a figure of 1,000. The bank pays no interest on small and medium deposits in current accounts. On some very large deposits, fixed deposits, and savings accounts it pays a variable but never very high rate of interest. Let us suppose that the average rate paid on various deposits is 3 percent, that is, 30 on 1,000. The bank, in its turn, will lend part of the money received in deposits, keeping only a minor part in liquid form to meet withdrawals. Let us suppose that the bank holds 200 in liquid form and lends 800 in various forms at an average interest rate of 8 percent which gives 64. At the year's end the bank's profit will be: 64 (interest received) – 30 (interest paid out) = 34. Like the industrial capitalist, the banker will relate this profit to the 100 originally invested. The gross rate of profit is thus: $\frac{34}{100} = 34\%$. The rate of profit is calculated on the capital of the capitalist, but the money the banker puts to work as capital is *other* peoples' money. "In interest-bearing capital," in Marx's words, "this automatic fetish, self-expanding value, money generating money . . . is potentially self-expanding value and is loaned out as such . . . . it becomes a property of money to generate value and yield interest. . . ." Behind this facade, however, the mystification of capital producing interest— "much as it is an attribute of pear trees to produce pears"[1]—lies the essential though not immediately visible reality that all capital is no more than the embodiment of past labor and that the value of such past labor can be transmitted and integrated into new value only by contact with living labor—new productive labor.

The fetish of interest-bearing capital is only a fantasy, yet it is so deeply implanted in the mind of all capitalists that they quite naturally distinguish two separate elements in the profit of any type of enterprise, in the belief that their capital is in itself capable of creating interest. The first part is the interest on the capital; the second is the surplus of profit (total profit less the interest on the capital), which is called the *entrepreneurial profit*.

If, in a given year, a capitalist makes a net profit of 20 percent on capital, and this capital loaned to others could have brought in 7 percent in interest over the same period, the capitalist will firmly—and mistakenly—conclude that capital brought in 7 percent interest and 13 percent entrepreneurial profit or remuneration for managerial work. In the mind of the capitalist this return or remuneration is justified by the fact that a well-managed enterprise makes more profit than one that is mismanaged.

It is beyond question that no enterprise can survive and flourish without the contribution of administration and management, which merits remuneration like any other work. Similarly, there can be no doubt that this work must be regarded as productive. Just as a skilled conductor is necessary to the best performance of an orchestra, so only competent management can efficiently coordinate the multiplicity of different tasks in a single enterprise. On the scale of a large enterprise, work is not so much the sum of individual inputs of labor as the intergated activity of a *collective worker*, from laborer to director, who creates surplus value indivisibly.

Thus no fundamental, eternal principle makes the management function inseparable from that of the capitalist. The functions of management and administration are, moreover, often entrusted to salaried personnel, however privileged these may be, and, in the United States, these even set the tone in the capitalist world. The economist John Kenneth Galbraith has observed that management and administration of the giant corporations is, more and more, detached from finance—which finds it advantageous to delegate them to a collective of high-powered technicians. This Galbraith describes as a "technostructure." This does not, however, prevent finance capital from gaining the famous entrepreneurial profit.

Above all it must not be forgotten that we are analyzing a system based on class antagonism—specifically between those workers who are direct producers and the owners of the means of production. In this situation the functions of management and administration are inseparable from those of oversight and oppression, which become repression pure and simple as soon as the confrontation of classes becomes sharper or more widespread. Management and administration in this context bear no relation to the organization of labor within a peaceful homogeneous collective worker. The entrepreneurial profit is thus no more justifiable than interest on capital. Both are mental constructs of a class masking the fundamental reality of the exploitation of labor by capital.

It remains to say a word about that other form of profit, rent on land. This will be described mainly for historical reasons since issues of agricultural landholding have declined, certainly in the advanced capitalist societies, with the decrease in the number of workers concerned (and many of these part time), in relation to the increasing number of industrial workers.

First, we must recall that working the land produces materials useful to society and generates value, and hence also surplus value, when it is performed within the capitalist mode of production and labor power is purchased for wages. Land itself is a productive factor which has no more inherent value than air or water and could only be assimilated by capital at the point where all usable cleared land had been privately appropriated. From that time in history land produced rent if rented or leased in a manner roughly similar to that by which money lent to an industrialist brought in interest. Thus rent on land is a special case of profit.

8
The Subdivision of Surplus Value:
An Apparent Paradox?

We saw earlier that in France out of eight hours' labor
something like five hours goes to produce surplus value,
which must, therefore, be enormous. If industrial capitalists were to keep the whole of surplus value for themselves
their profits would be of a quite different order from those
they actually realize.

Industrialists are, in fact, constrained to share this surplus value with others, and among these the state and commercial capital take the lion's share.

We have seen why the industrial capitalists have recourse to commercial capital for the distribution of their
products and how this benefits them. Obviously, they have
to pay for this service, which they do by relinquishing part
of the surplus value in the same way as the owners of a
building relinquish part of the price as commission to the
property agent who sells it. The matter is, however, more
complicated than that.

In practice, industrial capitalists often entrust the distribution of their products to general agents who, in turn,
sell it to wholesalers who again pass it on to retailers,
sometimes directly and sometimes through more specialized wholesalers. At the retail stage the commodities are
sold at their value, but at every stage a share of the value
has been levied by the relevant handler. Let us recall that
the value of a commodity is expressed as c + v + pl and

suppose that the part of fixed capital transfered in the commodity (c) comes to two, that the variable capital (v) or wages comes to three and that surplus value (pl) comes to five. In this arbitrary example the value of the commodity will be $2c + 3v + 5pl = 10$. At the final retail stage the commodity will be sold at this value and this cannot generally be otherwise. If the industrial capitalist sells the goods straight from the factory for eight, then the commercial agents at the various stages in the process of distribution will share two; two is therefore that part of surplus value (5) which the industrial capitalist has to relinquish to commercial capital as a whole. This sector takes its share of surplus value, but does not create any of it.

At the present time there is a tendency for the steps in the distribution process to decease owing to the growth of chain stores, large-scale outlets, and specialists in sales by mail order, all of which could reduce commercial capital's share of surplus value. On the other hand, commercial capital has expanded into market analysis, advertising agencies, etc., which have grown enormously. When all its claims are met, the commercial sector is certainly overall the greediest private claimant to that portion of surplus value which the industrial capitalist is obliged to relinquish.

The public sector—the state—however, is voracious too. The state has become the collector of a considerable volume of resources, since national budgets attract as much as one-fifth to one-fourth of the national income. Less than 10 percent of its receipts derive from taxes on company profits, so that the direct levy on the total national surplus value is modest. But some three-fourths of state receipts are derived from direct taxation of earnings and indirect taxes such as sales taxes, excise duties on liquor, tobacco, etc.

At first sight it would appear that such receipts are levied on the incomes of those concerned—that is, the wages and salaries of workers. Earlier we saw that a wage is equivalent to the value of labor power, that is, equal to the value of goods enabling this labor power to maintain and reproduce itself. We may recognize that certain state services—health and education—contribute to the training and maintenance of the labor power of the workers in general and conclude that the fraction of taxes required for the operation of these services is levied on the value of labor power.

No one, however, will believe that the army, the courts, the police, or many other facets of public administration are instruments of the state directed to the maintenance and reconstitution of the labor force. Neither their functions nor their costs have any connection with the value of labor power or with wages, although they seem to be levied on the latter. Thus we find that wages and salaries, as they are currently defined, fall into two parts: the wages or salaries proper, as we have scientifically defined them, with the addition of a portion of surplus value appropriated by the capitalists, which they have been constrained to add to real wages with a view to their transfer to the state in taxes. Thus both productive and nonproductive workers see a considerable volume of surplus value from all sorts of capitalist enterprises pass through their wages and salaries to the state. These can be seen to have the same basis as the costs of circulation referred to earlier and they can, therefore, only be ultimately derived from surplus value. Just as the part of surplus value transferred to the commercial sector provides it with the means for activity designed to increase total surplus value, so that part transferred to the bourgeois state provides the means to conduct the affairs of the nation in the interests of the class which has appropriated the surplus value and relinquished part of it to the state.

There are, however, other transfers of surplus value. We should remember that when industrial capitalists pay interest to banks or savers who have lent them money they are simply transferring part of the new surplus value whose generation has been facilitated by this money. In these days of increasingly complex economic life, enterprises of all sorts proliferate: for finishing, recycling, organization, management, research, etc., all used by capital and remunerated by a levy on surplus value.

There are yet others, often forgotten, who share in the benefits of surplus value and who present an especially interesting example because of their social repercussions. In every enterprise there are quite a number of managers and other senior staff who receive a variety of payments and perquisites, making them relatively very comfortably off.

When the workers in a factory or group of factories present demands or go on strike, they do not directly confront the owner or top officials, but some member of the senior staff specifically delegated for that task. They soon realize that such a person is almost always on the other side of the barricades and is the spokesperson and representative of capital. Part of this individual's high remuneration is in return for an effective contribution to the production of the enterprise, and the other part for services as representative and executive of the authority of the employer and agent of oppression and repression. This second part of the remuneration cannot in any way be treated as a salary and is levied on surplus value.

This analysis may apply not only to senior staff. The murder of a worker in a French Renault factory in 1972 drew attention to the fact that many enterprises employ such people as former military or police personnel, not to take part in production, but for supervision, espionage, and repression of one kind or another. The wages of such company police can only be explained as a levy on surplus value. These preliminary observations will be of help to our later analysis of social classes.

To summarize, industrial capital first appropriates all surplus value, but can only keep part, as it has to hand over the remainder to various persons and agencies. Commercial capital, banking capital, the bourgeois state, private savers—all who contribute to the enlargement of total surplus value—participate in the division of spoils. Thus they all have an interest in the growth of total surplus value which can only be brought about by increasing the exploitation of the working class or, more generally, all wage and salary earners. However, once maximum total surplus value has been generated, all compete for a larger slice of the cake. There are, for example, rivalries between industrial capital, finance capital, and commercial capital, and thus internal contradictions within the capitalist class. Such contradiction between sectors is tempered by the tendency for rates of profit to equalize, and can never be more than secondary to the fundamental contradiction between the entire, united, capitalist class and the proletariat and its allies. All capitalists have a necessary interest in increasing exploitation; it is in the interests of all workers to oppose it.

In general the number of workers employed in an enterprise tends to be stable or to grow very slowly; in some sectors, automation has led to declining numbers. Wages never rise at breakneck speed, but on the other hand machinery and industrial supplies are increasingly numerous, effective, and costly thanks to advances in science and technology. The industrial world is thus characterized by constant and rapid growth in the value of the equipment and supplies of enterprises while there are only small increments in the general wage level.

Let us recall our formula for the rate of capitalist profit: $\frac{pl}{c + v}$, in which "pl" is surplus value, "c" fixed capital and "v" variable capital. As a result of the trend we have discovered, "c" in the formula tends to increase much more rapidly than "v," a movement we have described as an increase in the organic composition of capital.

Let us suppose, for example, that in a particular enterprise in 1930 c = 200 and v = 50. For the sake of argument, we will assume the currency to have remained stable. It would then not be an exaggeration to suggest that by 1970 "c" would have risen to 850 (more than fourfold) and "v" from 50 to 150 (threefold). What, then, of "pl"? We know that surplus value is directly related to the value of labor power, that is to "v," and we can fairly hypothesize that in 1970, surplus value was worth twice "v" as it was in 1930. This gives us:

$$\text{rate of profit in 1930} = \frac{100\text{pl}}{200c + 50v} = 40\%$$

$$\text{rate of profit in 1970} = \frac{300\text{pl}}{850c + 150v} = 30\%$$

The rate of surplus value remaining constant, the markedly greater increase in fixed capital over variable capital caused a considerable fall in the rate of profit. The uninterrupted progress of science and technology leads to the general phenomenon of an increasing organic composition of capital throughout the economy. *The tendency of the average rate of profit to fall is, therefore, fundamental to the capitalist economy.*

Why, then, is this law defined as a "tendency"? Because like all economic laws, it arises from contradictory elements.

The struggle between opposites is universal, so that the phenomenon fundamental to this tendency is opposed by others which counteract it with more or less effect according to time and circumstances. Thus the falling rate of profit is a general tendency which is manifested with greater or lesser force as the pressure of scientific and technological innovation varies and meets with stronger or weaker counterpressures.

What are the counterpressures, what are the opposing factors? In our example above we postulated a constant rate of surplus value. In reality this is unlikely. Supposing that between 1930 and 1970 the rate of surplus value had risen from 2v to 2.5v, instead of remaining stable— we would have the following equation for the rate of profit:

$$\frac{375\text{pl}}{850c + 150v} = 37.5\%$$

The rise in the rate of surplus value would have taken up most of the fall in the rate of profit due to the rising organic composition of capital. Thus the classic defense of the capitalists against a fall in the rate of profit lies in the many forms of intensification of exploitation of labor which increase the rate of surplus value.

Trade with the underdeveloped countries is another factor operating in the same direction. Such trade enables the enterprises of the industrialized world to obtain raw materials such as oil and minerals at low prices, and so to reduce that part of constant capital required for their purchase. Moreover, the importation of certain major items of consumption tends to reduce the value of labor power, for it is certain that some increase in wages would ensue if coffee, cocoa, bananas, oranges, peanuts, etc., grew in industrial countries where they would cost more to produce. Finally, industrial products are usually sold to such countries at enhanced prices, providing superprofits. However, these opposing factors have a limited effect on the tendency of the rate of profit to fall.

Nowadays many economists lay greater stress on certain developments of modern capitalism which Marx obviously could not have taken into account. On the one hand, we have state intervention in economic life and, on the other, the expansion of many unproductive sectors usually described as the "tertiary sector." The latter may be unproductive and appear useless when judged by noncapitalist standards, yet they enhance the capitalist rate of profit. We will not at this point discuss this difficult and complex subject, but we can observe that the modern state puts various powerful restraints on the tendency of the rate of profit to fall. Among these are state pressure for the restructuring of industries and monopolistic concentrations, nationalization of sectors bringing little or no return (transport, communications) and ever increasing military and civil state orders on terms highly favorable to the industries concerned. The commercial sector is the foundation of the entire tertiary sector and, as we have seen, accelerates the circulation of capital, enabling industrial capital to produce more surplus value in a given time, and thus constitutes a major obstacle to the tendency of the rate of profit to fall.

Finally, we must not forget that the rate of profit which tends to fall is the "general" or average rate of profit, that is, the rate of profit for the whole economy. Wide variations may occur around the average rate depending on the nature of the industries concerned and, most of all, upon their size. Large firms and especially the giants (monopolies) are able to resist the tendency of the rate of profit to fall by more effective and varied means than are available to small and medium companies. This has been shown by experience and can even be demonstrated statistically.

It follows that the giant corporations have a far greater capacity to accumulate capital than do small or medium undertakings. This gap tends to widen, thereby increasing opportunities for monopolies to take over or control smaller undertakings which cannot survive alone but are preserved by amalgamation. The differential operation of the law of the tendency of the rate of profit to fall ultimately facilitates the accumulation and concentration of capital. Monopolies benefit by this trend and, for them, we must consider not only the rate of profit but also the volume of capital on which it is calculated, finding that the growth of the latter can compensate, or more, for the erosion of the former. Let us postulate a monopoly earning, in 1970, a rate of profit of 15 percent on $10 billion, giving a profit of $1.5 billion. Let us suppose that by 1974 its capital has been brought up to $20 billion though its rate of profit has fallen to 12 percent: it will realize a profit of $2.4 billion—far greater than that of 1970.

The law of the tendency of the rate of profit to fall has contradictory effects in conditions of monopolistic capital. By facilitating the concentration of capital it enables greater profits to be realized by monopolies even if the general rate of profit has fallen.

9
The Ups and Downs of Money: From Credit to Inflation

We begin, once again, with a brief retrospect. Earlier we saw that the value of a commodity only becomes apparent when it is exchanged for another. Barter, that most primitive form of exchange, has long since been abandoned. When our ancestors were faced with large numbers of commodities to exchange, they soon discovered a convenient measure for all values in a particular commodity or "general equivalent": *money*. From then on the value of a commodity was expressed in the number of units of the general equivalent for which it could be exchanged. Suppose the general equivalent to be gold and that a pair of shoes, for example, can be exchanged for ten grains of gold; the *price* of the shoes is then ten units of money. The price is simply the *monetary expression of value.*

The primary function of money is to be a *general measure of value*, in other words, *a standard of prices*. It has, however, other functions, of which the most important is that of facilitating circulation: Susan uses money to buy a coat from Paul; Paul uses the cash received to buy a transistor radio from Karen who, in turn, buys a case of canned fruit from Harry, etc. Some months or years later the transistor, the coat, and the canned fruit will have been used up. The sum of money originally put into circulation has facilitated the exchange and subsequent consumption

of these and many other commodities but the money itself has not been consumed. The money commodity performs the task of moving, passing from hand to hand, and
thus facilitating the exchange of commodities.

Money does, however, sometimes stop circulating.
There is the miser who amasses it for pleasure, but mostly
it is people like Susan, who save when they want to buy a
good coat but cannot afford it out of one month's salary;
they therefore put aside a certain amount each month until they have saved the price of the desired garment. Everyone does this for a whole range of things, including the
capitalists who put part of their profit into reserve accounts,
amortization funds, or future investments. Money is thus
also a means of hoarding. Circulation and hoarding are
the two contradictory functions of money, yet they are
linked in a dialectical manner. For it is hoarding or saving which enables a larger sum of money to be put into
circulation at a particular time for the purpose of an exchange of greater value.

It may be objected that credit makes all this avoidable.
That is illusory, for if Susan gets credit to enable her to
buy her coat at once that very credit will be money saved
by others. *Credit* is a system or series of processes where-
by money hoarded by all kinds of savers can be mobilized
in the service of the capitalist mode of production, and it
matters little whether it was saved toward an ultimate
goal or without a special purpose.

For instance, nowadays all big banks offer their customers fixed-term savings accounts. I deposit a large sum
of money for an agreed period (often from one to three
years) and at the end of that period the bank returns my
deposit plus interest at a rate higher than that available
for short-term deposits. Why does my bank so kindly pay
this extra interest? Banks are only kind when it profits
them. Because it knows that I will not withdraw my deposits until the agreed time, in the intervening period the
bank can use the money for short-term loans on which it
charges a higher rate of interest than it is paying me. These

credits will, therefore, be based on my savings or hoarding.

There are three major forms of credit, divided according to their purposes:

One form is *circulation credit*, which is usually short-term, as, for example, when a wholesale operation gets an advance on goods awaiting sale in its warehouse. A steel mill may have sold and delivered a large quantity of special steel to a metallurgical undertaking, but have obtained the order only by accepting payment three months later by means of bills maturing in ninety days. Fortunately, its bank will "discount" these bills, will pay out the value at once—charging a retainer or discount—and collect on the bills when they fall due. Circulation credit is always given in anticipation of expected payments and so accelerates the rate of circulation of capital, which as we know causes surplus value to increase. It is often effected by discounting commercial bills, as in the above example. It is also done by extending advances on current account, banking accounts being opened in the expectation that they will be overdrawn and then, quite properly, interest will be paid on the overdraft.

A second form of credit, *industrial or investment credit*, is long-term and usually concerns large sums, enabling enterprises to expand further and faster than their own capital would permit. A recent example was the amalgamation of two French iron foundries, bringing together the biggest iron founders of one industrial nation. The total cost of the combine was estimated at 7 billion francs, but the two participants were not worth more than 1 billion francs. The vast balance required was raised from the banks (4.1 billion francs), and the state (2.65 billion francs). This kind of credit is fundamentally an anticipation of the accumulation of productive capital, enabling total surplus value to be increased. Most banks insist on being able to oversee the operations of the management of borrowing firms, or even on holding share capital. This practice was a major factor in the growth of *investment banks* during the nineteenth century. These financial establishments specialize in investing in numerous and various undertakings and in gaining control over many of them.

Everybody knows about the third form, *consumer credit*, which has expanded at so fantastic a rate in recent years. "Impulse buying," as it is called, created a real boom in the production of consumer durables by suddenly making potential and fairly distant demands materialize today or tomorrow. Such credit also gives rise to anticipated demand and shortens the time required for the circulation of capital.

To sum up, in all its forms credit is an instrument in the service of capital. It operates by seeking out all reserves of liquid money, great or small, and rounding them up for the coffers of private and public finance houses (commercial banks, savings banks, deposit accounts, etc.), and by so doing builds them into money capital on a special scale for the benefit of the capitalist mode of production. Circulation credit, investment credit, or consumer credit all operate to accelerate the cycles and economic processes of capitalism, thus increasing the volume of surplus value. It follows that credit must be put on the list of factors operating against the tendency of the rate of profit to fall and added to those other factors briefly described in the preceeding chapter.

Let us return to money. We saw that the precious metals gold and silver quickly established themselves as commodity-money. To facilitate their use states allocated to themselves the right to strike them into coins worth a certain number of monetary units. These were of certain value and circulated easily. With the conquest of distant lands and the discovery of America, individuals who owned many gold or silver ingots began to deposit them in a bank for safety. In exchange the bank would give them a paper acknowledging the deposit, known as a "bank note." Then, for convenience, instead of issuing a note for a total deposit of gold worth say, 5,380 units of money, the bank would hand over ten notes worth 500, three worth 100, one worth 50, and three 10s. This facilitated the transfer of these notes from hand to hand, and any person holding a 100-unit share knew that the bank would exchange it for 100 units of gold at any time.

Later the custom was gradually established that banks entitled to issue money would issue paper notes backed by their own stock of gold in addition to metal coins. These notes became *fiduciary* money (from a Latin world for confidence), because their effectiveness depended on confidence in the issuing institution which guaranteed their convertibility into precious metal. We know, however, that one should never have too much confidence in those whose business is the manipulation of money. In fact, the national banks issuing money soon realized that individuals were less and less often trying to change their bank notes into gold coins. At the same time the total volume of trade had grown so much (money having lost much of its power) that the gold reserves of a nation would have been insufficient for it all. So the national banks stopped striking gold coins and began to print notes far in excess of the value of the gold in their vaults and then they all, at some point in time, simply abandoned the convertibility of notes into gold. Money had ceased to be a commodity and become a symbol or sign without intrinsic value.

While money as such was changing in this way, other monetary forms appeared and flourished. Some of these arose from the credit system and were mentioned in discussing that topic. Thus a credit note or bill of exchange, which is an undertaking to pay a certain sum at a certain time, can be endorsed from one person to another several times and so circulate like a bank note.

Above all it was the check which came into widespread use and grew into a substitute for money. I sign a check for 100 units in favor of a store from which I have made a purchase. The owners will not go to my bank to collect their 100 units, for they have their own bank account, in which they can deposit my check. The two banks settle the matter by simply writing the transaction into their accounts. There has been a money settlement, but it has not been through the medium of any bank notes. Checks, bills of exchange or credit, advances on current account (overdrafts), and settlements by endorsement on accounts are all forms of money other than cash.

In modern times the total means of payment in circulation in a country is composed partly of bank notes issued by the appropriate institution, and for the rest, all the other forms of money we have mentioned. There is far more money involved in the latter group. In any case, the total volume of means of payment of all kinds has the social function of enabling the exchange, at their value, of all commodities offered on the market, taking into account the average rate of circulation of the various forms of money. If these change hands on average five times a year they should amount to approximately one-fifth of the total value of goods exchanged during the year. It may happen that the total value of money (or forms of money) in circulation seems to be insufficient. In such cases it is easy to create more money. It happens much more frequently that there is a persistant excess of money—and this situation is described as *inflation*.

The state is often directly responsible for such a situation. Since it controls the issue of bank notes it is greatly tempted to make the money process work faster when it is short of resources for what it judges to be necessary expenditure. When this happens the volume of money grows without a corresponding growth in the volume of commodities available for exchange. The overall value of commodities produced remains the same, but will be expressed in prices through a larger quantity of money. There follows a general rise in the level of prices, a fall in the purchasing power of bank notes, or even a *de facto* devaluation of the currency.

The depreciation of money caused by an unwarranted issue of bank notes may lead to rising prices. The reverse, however, has occurred much more frequently in recent times; that is, a rise in prices causes an increase in the volume of money and its depreciation. This can be described as the fundamental cause of an inflationary situation which tends to become permanent and coterminous with the capitalist mode of production.

The protagonists of this mode of production attribute inflation following price increases to wages rising faster than productivity. Let us recall that we represented the value of a commodity by the formula $M = c + v + pl$. If all conditions of production remain unchanged, it is obvious that wage increases will cause "v" to rise, followed by "M," and that this will work through to the price which is the monetary expression of value. This argument assumes that surplus value (pl) is unalterable and sacred. If this assumption is rejected, wages can rise even faster than productivity without causing prices to rise, on condition that there is a corresponding fall in surplus value. However simplified it may be, this reasoning is sound and serves only to highlight a fundamental truth: inflation in general, and more especially the current variety set off by price increases, is not really a technical problem but is an expression of the essential class struggle. When the efforts of the workers bring about any appreciable increase in their purchasing power, and other conditions are unchanged, the capitalists cannot maintain, and still less improve, the rate of surplus value unless they raise prices and bring about inflation. Moreover, they usually get in first: prices are increased without economic justification, while wages are not allowed to rise faster than productivity—all this for the sole purpose of increasing surplus value.

This has become one of the basic problems of monopoly capitalism and merits further discussion. It is, however, more appropriate to specialized works.

10
The Uncontrolled Accumulation
of Capital and Economic Crises

Earlier we described the process of the circulation of capital as follows: the capitalist's original money capital is first transformed into productive capital which, by the end of the productive phase, has given rise to commodity capital. Finally, through exchange, this latter reproduces money capital, enabling the cycle to begin again, and so on and so on.

It follows that the process of commodity production is also a process of *reproduction of capital*. The amount of money which appears at the end of the cycle is, however, greater than the amount put in at the beginning: it has been increased by surplus value, that is, the value generated by the surplus labor of the proletariat and appropriated by the capitalist.

Two hypotheses can be constructed on these facts: (1) The capitalist consumes the whole surplus value, which is thus transformed into income and dissipated by personal or family spending. In this case the capital put back into production is exactly the same as that put in at the beginning of the cycle. The capital has simply been reproduced, value for value, and production can continue only on exactly the same scale as before. This is called *simple reproduction.*

(2) The capitalist uses only part of surplus value as rev-

enue to be consumed, and devotes the rest to increasing productive capital. In this case production can continue on a larger scale. This is called *enlarged reproduction.*

It is obvious that competition between capitalists turns them away from simple reproduction and leads to a preference for enlarged reproduction, since the latter alone enables capitalist development. Enlarged reproduction is, therefore, the general rule and leads to the phenomenon of *the accumulation of capital.*

Marx used the term *concentration* of capital as a more precise term for the accumulation of capital within an enterprise by the internal operations of enlarged reproduction. This concentration of capital varies from enterprise to enterprise: some develop and concentrate capital faster than others, and then tend to buy out or take over weaker enterprises in order to accelerate and consolidate their lead. This movement creates a trend for the greater to absorb the smaller and for weak capital to be swallowed up to enlarge the strong. Marx called this the centralization of capital into fewer and fewer hands. Nowadays the term concentration is preferred to describe both these movements of capital which are, moreover, dialectically related: concentration leads to centralization which, in turn, facilitates internal accumulation since large undertakings usually enjoy a higher rate of profit than small ones.

The trend toward the amalgamation of enterprises and the centralization of capital is not always furthered by big firms buying up and taking over smaller ones; two enterprises of similar size may also amalgamate by agreement the better to face competition. In this case neither can be said to dominate or absorb the other. It is, however, very common for a large or very large enterprise to be satisfied with "taking control" of one or more smaller enterprises, allowing them to continue as legal entities, rather then buying them up outright. Taking control of an enterprise entails acquiring as much of its capital as is necessary to be its unquestioned master and make it play its part in the expansionist strategy of the entire monopolistic group. The proportion of capital necessary for such control varies widely from case to case.

At this stage it should be stressed, however, that accumulation does not only constitute the reproduction of the productive process and reproduction of capital on a greater scale, but also the *reproduction of capitalist social relations.* The reproduction of capital puts the workers back into precisely those conditions which enabled this reproduction: as sellers of the same labor power for the benefit of the same capital which extracts from them surplus value. Capital accumulates more rapidly than the proletarian class increases and is constantly concentrating into fewer and fewer hands, thus increasing its effectiveness in the class struggle. Finally, it is strengthening its strangle hold on the state as monopolization progresses. All these developments aggravate productive relations and, more generally, social relations between classes.

Accumulation of capital is, however, one of the most fundamental characteristics of present-day capitalism. At times when capital investment is increasing faster than production, some people actually speak of surplus accumulation of capital. Actually the enlarged production of capital does not progress with the regularity of clockwork. The accumulation of capital has its ups and downs; we have all heard of recessions, crises, and the opposite phenomenon of "booms." Capitalism developed enormously in the nineteenth century and yet crises (or depressions) occurred at about ten-year intervals. The twentieth century has not escaped; the deepest and the last, of global extent, was the Great Depression of 1929-1933.

The periodic occurence of depressions gave rise to the notion of the "economic cycle": capitalism is supposed to develop not in a straight line but in a fluctuating movement with more or less regular rhythm. The cycle can be broadly described (but not explained) as follows: a period of prosperity is suddenly followed by rapid decline accompanied by bankruptcies, unemployment, falling prices, and vanishing profits. Then the crisis is followed by a depression: the economy cruises along in a state of general paralysis with production at a very low level. Finally, a recovery begins, not suddenly, like the beginning of the crisis but slowly progressing in the reverse direction. This recovery usually gains speed and ends up in a fresh boom characterized by rapid growth of production, exchange, investment, etc. Activity generally reaches a higher level than before the depression, for the latter generates the conditions for a rise in the average rate of profit. This goes on until the economy becomes what is sometimes called "overheated": the engines of the economy race, overproduction appears, the economic machine breaks down, and crisis has come again.

Of course, the above is a sketch in very broad strokes and no two crises are, in practice, exactly alike. However, the features common to all crises impel us to ask the following questions: (1) What is the general cause of economic crises, that is, the breakdown of the mechanism of the accumulation of capital? (2) How can we explain the absence of a general crisis since 1933?

Both questions are difficult to answer. One cannot answer the first without turning to Marx's own analysis, in which he observes that all production of material goods is necessarily divided into two main parts:

Section 1 serves to produce the means of production, or productive goods (productive installations and equipment, machinery, raw materials and supplies, etc.); in other words, all the goods which are used *in the production of other goods.*

Section 2 serves to produce consumer goods; that is, all the various products which human beings consume, slowly or quickly, to satisfy their needs.

For example, there is machinery (smelters, rolling mills, and so on) for the manufacture of aluminum. Aluminum is the product of a certain means of production, yet is itself a means of production, for instance in the manufacture of food cans. But these cans are not further transformed: they are simply filled with baked beans or frankfurters, whereupon they and their contents become consumer goods as in Section 2. We could take endless examples and see that, quickly or slowly, directly or indirectly, the products of Section 1 are transformed into Section 2 products, and reach their final destination in consumption by human beings.

Human beings do not produce things at random, but create objects to satisfy their needs and desires—in the final analysis in order to *consume* them. Thus the requirements of Section 2 order the development of Section 1. However, innovations occurring in Section 1 may lower the prices of some goods in Section 2, thus leading to an expansion in their consumption. To put it another way, there is a close and reciprocal relationship between the development of Section 1 and that of Section 2. The accumulation of capital could not proceed smoothly if these respective developments were not in harmony.

Marx laid down the conditions required and rules to be observed if the reproduction of capital was to be crisis-free. His algebraic formulae are too complex to discuss in detail, but the following is a general outline of their content.

The material products of human labor are classified in Section 1 or 2 according to their use value or actual use. It is use value which motivates the exchange of goods. (I only buy a given product because it is of use to me or I believe it to be so.) But, on the other hand, it is the exchange value, expressed as price, which determines the conditions of this exchange and is sometimes a necessary condition for it: I cannot buy a commodity I need if I do not have the necessary purchasing power. Marx founded his analysis and descriptions on a consideration of the reciprocal relations of use value and exchange value.

For the products of both Sections 1 and 2 there must be a correlation between the quantity of goods offered for exchange and what is called "effective demand." Purchasing power capable of bringing about an exchange of all the goods offered on the market must also be immediately available purchasing power. In practice purchasing power available at a given time rarely corresponds with that effectively distributed (wages), or realized (surplus value), at that same time, because credit and saving anticipate or hold back the point in time at which purchasing power will be used. All this is said to illuminate the fact that a close correspondence between a certain amount of available goods and a certain amount of equally available monetary resources can only be obtained by playing correctly within certain rules and by the maintenence of certain equilibria (economic, financial, monetary). The equilibrium between Sections 1 and 2 is fundamental.

Within the capitalist mode of production, production is private and regulated by the laws of conflict and competition. The search for maximum profit leads to unequal development (within sectors and between them, between regions and between countries), which is a constant feature of the system. The engine of production is profit for the industrial entrepreneur, and not the harmonious development of the economic system as a whole. On the other hand, the rules whose observation could maintain the necessary balance relate to the economy as a whole and not only to industrial enterprises. However formally such rules might be enacted in law, they could never be strictly applied in a competitive economy. In fact they are not even enacted, for the classical bourgeois state which alone could do this is a class state, an expression of capital and by its very nature at the service of capital and not in the service of the general economy. Given these conditions the state can, at best, ensure a compromise between the primordial needs of capital and the necessity to maintain the engine of the general economy, failing which the interests of capital itself would be at risk. From day to day it tries to juggle the imbalances which appear. Up to the Second World War, however, they regularly did occur and often crossed the threshold into crisis.

This seems to contradict the sense of the second question: How can we explain the absence of a general crisis since 1933? Let us be clear: since the Second World War there has been no really deep crisis affecting the whole or a great part of the capitalist world. However, many countries have experienced more or less serious recessions, followed or preceded by periods of rapid growth. The United States has had its economic "booms," Germany and Italy their "miracles" (sandwiched between more or less deep recessions). France has experienced similar, if less marked, fluctuations. The United Kingdom is in a fairly settled depression, while Japan, on the contrary, has had a long, relatively stable period of growth. It could, therefore, be postulated that world capitalist development has continued unequal in time and space.

The recessions and depressions described have not reached the full proportions of a true crisis because the imbalances inherent in capitalist development constitute a tendency which can be counteracted by certain other factors. The most outstanding of these is the new role of the state. Until the Second World War capitalist states were not equipped with adequate means of economic intervention but have, since then, acquired such means: credit, money, prices, direct and indirect economic subsidies, foreign trade, differential tax policies, etc., which they have learned to use more or less effectively. The imperfect instruments of economic planning have in the medium term been applied in an effort to create conditions in which the inevitable imbalances will be less dangerous. Some states have become the employers and directors of essential public productive sectors (energy, transport). They can to some extent influence economic and social phenomena and cushion the economy against certain shocks. They can use various means to act directly on the movement, investment, and concentration of capital, and on the restructuring of industry. It is hard to underestimate the effect of a state budget of more than one-fifth of the national product and the value of civil and military expenditure, in staving off crises. Vast accumulations of capital are one of the characteristics of present-day capitalism and one of its major problems is the profitable utilization of new capital. Powerful armaments industries offer direct outlets to such capital and stimulate the opening up of others. The customer being the state—"their" state, in fact—prices are paid which allow superprofits to be made and work against the tendency for the rate of profit to fall. Finally, through the wages and salaries they distribute such industries create additional purchasing power not balanced by a corresponding increase in consumer goods.

There are certain new aspects of capitalist development itself which act as a defense against crises over and above the role of the state. The new technological revolution combined with fierce competition leading to monopolization makes the replacement of equipment and supplies much more rapid than in the past. This shortens the economic cycle and prevents depressions from developing to full crises and also creates continuing expansion in the production of Section 1. This expansion requires a larger labor force, increasing the purchasing power distributed by Section 1 which, in turn, generates development of the production of Section 2. The development of the latter is further accelerated by new features of what is called the "consumer society": endless modifications of products themselves or their presentation; various models of all kinds of equipment; new products and slight variants, under new brand names; the extension of the use of gadgets—all conspiring to turn human beings into consumer robots through the degrading effects of pervasive advertising and the diversification of forms of credit designed to hasten or create potential effective demand.

This consumer society inevitably inflates what is called the tertiary sector and more especially the commercial sector in its widest sense. Thus, excess capital can be invested outside the productive sector and there employ extra workers whose purchasing power leads to expansion in the production of Section 2. All this contributes to the realization of increasing surplus value and the consequent pursuit of capital accumulation.

Whether these factors and direct actions against crises derive from the state or from new forms of capitalist development, they in no way affect the central nature of the system, or the fundamental effect of the laws that control it. They may accelerate or slow down certain tendencies but cannot transform such tendencies and imbalances into their opposites. The inherent contradictions are still present in the system.

Most of the defenses against crises have attendant dangers: they have inflationary effects. Expenditure on armaments creates effective demand without a proportionate increase in the quantity of commodities available for exchange, and the expansion of the tertiary sector can only bring about a corresponding increase in commodity production in the long run. Credit aggravates these inflationary effects. The phase of capitalism which has succeeded in juggling with various imbalances has in the process itself created a new and considerable danger: *permanent and general inflation.* Together with the collapse of the international monetary order, this condition is one of great peril for the system.

11
Monopoly Power:
The New Face of Imperialism

We have seen that the accumulation of capital does not benefit all capitalists through equal distribution, but rather leads to the concentration of capital in the hands of a privileged minority. Concentration is the outcome of competition. In the practice of competition, certain enterprises are proved stronger than others. The powerful absorb or subordinate the weak and thus remove competitors. The new giants, however, meet even more intense competition, at a higher level, from enterprises which have also grown by concentration. Competition gives rise to concentration and the latter leads back to competition. Again we find the dialectical movement governing the development of economies and societies.

Lenin made a special study of the first great movement toward concentration in the capitalist world, which occurred at the end of the last century. The concentration of capital finds its most notable expression in the tendency to monopoly. A monopoly, in the fullest sense, would be an industry which has absolute control of an entire market. Such enterprises are extremely rare in the real world and the term monopoly is used for large-scale corporations which control a significant slice of a particular market and strive to expand to dominate the whole. In Western Europe, during the last third of the nineteenth century, such monopolies grew so rapidly that national markets soon appeared too small for them. Customs barriers hindered real competition between British, French, and German monopolies, in their respective national territories; on the other hand, there were many countries, some vast, in Asia and Africa which were still outside the capitalist system or on its fringes. Moreover, many of these had very poor defenses. The principal West European states, sharing the objectives of their own capitalists, launched or re-launched a powerful new wave of colonial conquests designed to provide their respective monopolies with vast reserved or privileged "economic space."

Thus was imperialism, "the highest stage of capitalism," born. Imperialism is nothing more than capitalism which has reached a given size and scale, entailing, in turn, qualitative mutations and transformations of its resources and methods. From the first, the colonized lands offered imperialism some raw materials (oil), and some products for mass consumption but, above all, they provided an outlet for commodity exports and the investment of capital which was accumulating so rapidly that it was difficult to apply at home. Imperialism was to modify the effect of imbalances inherent in the capitalist system and the tendency of the rate of profit to fall.

Rivalries between imperialist nations are, on the other hand, exacerbated by colonialism. Some had more colonies than others, and the partition of the world was virtually complete by the end of this century, leaving the less fortunate no recourse but to seek a redivision of the spoils by violence. Therein lie the root causes of the First World War (1914-1918), whose end saw Africa repartitioned at the expense of a vanquished Germany. Between the two world wars the capitalist world was somewhat stagnant with exports of commodities and capital stable and the movement toward concentration slow and even.

During the period following the end of the Second World War in 1945, a variety of major changes occurred. The world capitalist economy regained momentum through necessary reconstruction, enhanced its efficiency through a new technical and scientific revolution, and learned to use various palliatives and buffers to prevent recessions and depressions degenerating into general crises. In these conditions, growth was rapid, exports of commodities and capital increased prodigiously, and rates of capital accumulation reached new heights, engendering a similarily unprecedented movement toward concentration. This development began in the United States and the United Kingdom and extended to Japan and some West European countries; it came rather late to France where it became equally marked by the late 1960s. New mergers, regroupments, etc., are constantly being announced, often with capital foreign to the country concerned in control or participation.

During the same period, an irresistible movement for political emancipation spread like wildfire through Africa and Asia, where most countries gained nominal independence peacefully or through violent struggles. This independence is termed nominal because the subordination and pillage of what is called the Third World continues. The form has simply been adapted to the new situation of neocolonialism and is usually operated through indigenous governments which are virtually at the beck and call of imperialist masters.

The imperialists and monopolists of the present are the successors of those which flourished at the beginning of the century, but there are a number of important differences.

With reference to the monopolies, capital accumulation and concentration have not been specific to the industrial sector, but from the nineteenth century onward have also characterized banking, giving great impetus to the growth of *investment banks*. These are specialist banks which concentrate on investing their capital in a great variety of different undertakings, but with special emphasis on industry and always seeking to gain control. The barrier between banking capital and industrial capital has thus begun to break down. As the first form of capital penetrated the latter more and more deeply, it became *finance capital*. Conversely, and more recently, many giant corporations of industrial origin have begun to invest a major proportion of their accumulated profits in enterprises operating in quite unrelated sectors. They function very much like investment banks and are called *holding companies.*

Financiers who direct investment banks and also rule expensive capitalist empires enjoy a form of power which has long been described as *oligarchy.* Now this form also applies to the capitalists of holding companies and is extending to the large capitalist corporations which are diversifying their activities. In fact, the financial, commercial, and industrial sectors overlap one another more and more.

Thus the oligarchy consists of a small number of very big capitalists whose direct and indirect power enables them to dominate the economy. Their real power is, moreover, much greater than is reflected in the volume of capital they own. Small and medium shareholders do not usually attend meetings, or exercise proxy votes, and so the major shareholders can do as they like. A company may be controlled by the person or persons holding a minority of shares—30 percent, 20 percent, or even less. The game of acquiring subsidiaries reduces the holdings required for control still further.

Let us suppose the average number of shares required for control to be 33 percent throughout one financial group. If company A in this group, controlled by 33 percent of its capital, in turn holds 33 percent of the shares in subsidiary company A', the latter can be controlled by the group through 33 percent of 33 percent, or 11 percent. And there is nothing to prevent subsidiary A' from setting up a *further* subsidiary. This is why the capital of investment banks and holding companies is often invested through a complicated network of subsidiaries. Thus, capital of 1,000 units might control an empire of 5,000, 10,000, or more. In 1973 the Suez Finance Company and the Bank of Indochina admitted to joint control of 300 to 400 companies!

Industrial and banking monopolies show an increasing tendency to transcend national barriers and are often called multinationals—which is not quite accurate. These are large corporations and investment banks whose activities extend beyond the frontiers of their country of origin and often penetrate the whole world. Two hundred of the world's largest corporations have affiliates in twenty or more countries. The Compagnie Générale d'Electricité is a French company which is only a modest international monopoly, yet its 1969 report stated that it is present in more than one hundred countries. So too, Citibank, N.A., a New York-based commercial bank, reports branches, affiliates, and subsidiaries in over a hundred countries worldwide.

It is broadly true to say that most major companies, and almost all monopolies, are transnational. The most remarkable transnationals are those industrial monopolies with productive enterprises scattered about the most diverse countries throughout the world. The French aluminum monopoly, Péchiney, is an interesting example: in 1972 44 percent of its production took place in France and 56 percent in five other countries from the United States to the Cameroons.

Firms can be not only transnational, but truly multinational, if their capital is drawn from different countries. Such companies are often joint subsidiaries of a number of national monopolies from different countries. Multinationals are still fairly uncommon in industrialized countries but are, on the other hand, becoming increasingly numerous in Third World countries.

There are other forms of partial association or international cooperation between monopolies of different nations. What stands out from the points outlined is the general tendency for monopolies, alone or in combination, to spread their tentacles over the entire world market, always with the purpose of accelerating the accumulation/concentration of capital. It is also their desire to trade as freely between Chicago, Paris, and Singapore as between two cities in one state; and to set up factories in Montreal, São Paulo, or Abidjan with the same ease they would have in a single industrial country. To this end they aspire to a world economic and political order which would free the movement of capital and commodities and regulate currencies and their circulation. The European Common Market is simply a regional forerunner of such a world order. The crises which frequently occur in this field are an indication of the enormous difficulties in the way of achieving such a world order (even without taking into account the possibility of revolution intervening). As we have seen, every tendency clashes with its opposite; every development is contradictory within itself. However, the dynamics of a situation are best understood by seeking out the dominant tendency. Within monopoly capitalism today this is the aspiration for an integrated world order.

There is no longer much argument about the fact that international monopolies pillage the Third World in various ways. But debate continues as to the extent of the proceeds of this pillage in relation to the vast surplus value extorted from workers in the "developed" countries, and as to its effects on the system's prospects for survival.

Trade is the vehicle for one important form of pillage. We know that the value of a commodity is determined by the amount of labor socially necessary to produce it, and that the value of the labor force is represented by the value of the goods required to maintain and renew it. It is recognized, however, that the value of such goods is infinitely lower in underdeveloped countries, where it is a little more than a "physiological minimum" (the exact amount indispensable for subsistence and work), and that in developed countries it combines a complex of individual and social expenditures. It follows that, even if one were to calculate on a basis of equal productivity, which is unreal, African, Asian, and South American labor is at a far lower price than that of Europeans and North Americans. To give a concrete instance, if our coffee, cocoa, bananas, etc., could be produced in Europe or North America they would be much higher in price. It is generally true that the underdeveloped countries export goods that are relatively undervalued, while those of the developed world are overvalued. This is known as *unequal exchange*.

The financial value of unequal exchange is almost incalculable. At best, one can make a few rough estimates. It is, however, possible to measure its progress; for it is progressing in a negative direction. It is described as the "deterioration in the terms of trade" which are, for any country, the relationship between the average value of a ton of goods exported and a ton imported. Thus we know statistically that the Third World countries, taken together, had to export 15 percent more of their raw products in 1970 than had been necessary in 1956 to import the same amount of manufactured goods. In producing this 15 percent of their exports in 1970 they were working not for their own development but "for the King of Prussia," that is, for the monopolies and the imperialist economies.

Though the amount so extracted is vast on the Third World scale, it makes only a modest contribution to the coffers of the imperialist economies, for only 19 percent of the total external trade of all the advanced countries together is conducted with the entire Third World, or 2.25 percent of their gross product. And this proportion is declining.

The capital the imperialist monopolies have invested in the Third World countries, on the other hand, drains them of large profits. Very little is reinvested (less than 15 percent), the bulk of it being repatriated to the imperialist countries. In 1970-1971 an annual average of $8.8 billion were so repatriated; this was a significantly large sum for the Third World, in excess of all overseas aid received during the same period. Yet the amount represents only some 2 percent of internal savings in the rich countries—to whom it is, therefore, of little significance.

To sum up, superprofits from unequal trade, together with those from capital invested in the Third World and any other forms of pillage, have a countervailing effect on the tendency of the rate of profit in imperialist countries to fall, and this may have been important in the past. Now it is only marginal, and these superprofits cannot be regarded as the safety valve of the imperialist system.

It seems that imperialism's continued interest in the

Third World stems from something else. Today the whole industrial edifice of imperialism rests on the energy (fuel oil) and industrial raw materials of the Third World. In 1975 it was only possible for the developed industrial countries to satisfy their global needs by turning to the underdeveloped nations for the following proportion of their supplies:

50 percent of requirements in fuel oil
35 percent of requirements in iron
50 percent of requirements in bauxite
85 percent of requirements in chrome, manganese, antimony
70 percent of requirements in cobalt
90 percent of requirements in tin
45 percent of requirements in copper

All the major industrial countries are dependent in this way, and not only those which lack natural resources, such as Britain, Germany, Italy, and Japan, but also those which were originally well endowed, such as the United States and, to a lesser degree, France. The latter was once the world's biggest producer of bauxite, and is now sixth, producing only 5 percent. The United States is still the world's biggest producer of fuel oil and copper (but reserves are beginning to dwindle), but even so it has to import ever increasing quantities of both.

Being common to all, this dependency tends to strengthen the urge for imperialist integration aimed at establishing a firm, multinational grip on the indispensable wealth of the Third World. This is why corporations built on multinational capital proliferate in the field of extraction and preliminary processing of minerals from the underdeveloped areas—especially Africa. Such corporations are still relatively uncommon elsewhere. The monopolies of the new imperialism are quite firm about their preference for a Third World where natural wealth would be accessible to all, with trade and capital movement as free as possible for all. The raw materials of the Third World are the vital safety valve of the system and of each national imperialism; and so all, including imperialist states themselves, are basically agreed to maintain and, if possible strengthen, the structures enabling them to dominate and exploit the peoples of Africa, Asia, and Latin America. State-to-state aid to the Third World is now almost fully coordinated with economic interests. It serves to open the way for private capital and to insure the subservience of so many indigenous authorities. Intent to control the Third World is now a dominant tendency of monopolistic capitalism. In some fields it is still weak, but it is already acting with some effectiveness and little hindrance to subordinate the peoples of the underdeveloped countries and pillage the fruits of their labor. In reaction, however, the consciousness of the masses in these countries is stirring and the voice of protest is making itself heard.[1]

12
The Demystification of the State:
The Reality of Bourgeois Democracy

In the distant past, people came together in families, clans, and larger groupings, and the organization of labor and social life flowed from general agreement founded on customs born of experience and respected by all. Work was peacefully divided in the system known as the "private commune" because no one exploited his or her neighbor. The community did not depend on specialists or specialized organizations for the coordination of its functions, and no one was a full-time specialist.

Everything changed when exploitation appeared—as, for example, in slavery. As soon as one group or class within a society had successfully used force to dominate another, and appropriate its labor, social antagonisms made it impossible to achieve a general consensus, and it became necessary to create the institutions and instruments capable of giving permanence to a society which engenders and maintains internal conflicts. Thus, institutions are necessarily restrictive and oppressive, organizational and administrative, and, as soon as the new type of society develops, they constitute the *state*.

Thus the state is not as old as human society. It is a product only of class society. Indeed, the state became necessary to maintain the dominance of one human group over another, and so cannot be for the benefit of all, exploiters and exploited alike, but only an instrument in the hands of the oppressors. The state was not born of common consent at a certain stage in human development and then appropriated by the dominant class for its own ends. On the contrary, it is the very creation of the dominant class.

We have seen that material conditions of production and the mode of production are the economic *infrastructure*, or material base, of any society. It is this infrastructure which determines morality, law, culture and ideology, and the organs of society and public life—in a word, the *superstructure* of which the state is, in fact, the central organ. So the state is a reflection of the economic infrastructure. More precisely, it reproduces economic relations of domination and exploitation in its own sphere, which embraces the whole range of institutions controlling a nation. But the dialectic teaches us to look at all the different and contradictory aspects presented by every phenomenon. And, indeed, while the state is undoubtedly a reflection of the infrastructure, it is not a *passive* reflection. Once created and brought to life, the state becomes a specific force with a life of its own, and may react upon the infrastructure that gave birth to it, even while reflecting it. This explains some seeming ambiguities we will encounter later.

What we have learned so far shows us that the state expresses the domination of a minority class, and is its chosen instrument of oppression. It follows that the main purpose of the state is to *legalize violence*. If the use of violence were presented as the naked manifestation of the right of the strong, resistance would be such as to imperil society itself. The use of violence must, therefore, be presented as a manifestation of ordinary law, or even better, eternal law, whether of human or divine origin. The primary role of the state is thus to disguise the law of the strong as a law purporting to guarantee the good of each and all: falsification is one of its essential weapons.

The state is essentially conceived of as permanent, and it endures as long as the dominance of a class, and hence the mode of production which ensures its supremacy, exists. *Government*, on the other hand, is simply a group of people called on to operate the state for a given period, which is often quite short. This distinction may seem obvious, but it must be remembered that claims have been made at various times that a "new state" had been created. When Pétain took power in France during the Second World War he claimed that his "French state" was a new state, and he was believed by many. Twenty years later De Gaulle claimed to have "reformed" the state to the point of having changed its nature, and he also was believed by many (but not necessarily the same people).

A social democratic movement may be brought to office by powerful mass support, with quite different intentions; yet, if it accommodates to the existing state machine, it can achieve no more than the management of the bourgeois state with a more democratic orientation. From this it follows that a "socialist alternative" can be realized only by putting an entirely new state into the place of the old bourgeois state, since the new socialist mode of production must lead to the creation of different productive relations which will insure the predominance of a different class: the workers.

We shall now take a closer look at the state in general and, more especially, the monopoly capitalist state which at present confronts us in so many parts of the world.

The bourgeois state serves two purposes. Often the most conspicuous of these is the establishment and operation of the means of *coercion and repression*. No less important, though less obvious, is its part in organizing bourgeois democracy: that is, the combination of institutions, rules, and laws which disguise the oppression of the workers by the capitalist class and present a false front of equality. These two roles are interdependent and are only separated here for purposes of analysis.

The army and police are in the forefront of the instruments of repression at the disposal of the state. Once antagonistic classes appeared in society, it became impossible to entrust arms and the function of defense to all, since the oppressed majority might turn its arms against the oppressors. Thus permanent professional armies became the rule and the use of conscription was limited. The bourgeois state had recourse to military service for all only when the citizen soldier had been ideologically conditioned by a travesty of patriotism and, when called up, could be slotted into a professional army whose devotion was unconditional and whose discipline was inescapable.

The armies of the bourgeois state are at the service of the ruling capitalist class: in external conflicts, usually born of interimperialist rivalry (the First World War); in attempts to drown popular uprisings in blood (the Paris Commune, the intervention in Russia 1917-1920); in the past to conquer colonies, and nowadays to rush to the aid of servile neocolonialist governments (France in Gabon and Chad, and the United States in Taiwan and Vietnam); and, finally, to break strikes or mass demonstrations (Paris 1968, Chicago 1968).

The police of various countries have been used so freely, on such a scale, and have acted so violently that there is no further need to stress the part they play in the service of the state—they have come to be its very symbol.

The judiciary, courts, and prisons are all part of the repressive apparatus available to the state. Apart from the laws, which we shall discuss later, this apparatus practices *de facto* social discrimination, privileges being made available to the rich (and/or white): by their ability to buy the best defense, or to buy corrupt officials; by the better conditions they enjoy if sentenced; by prejudice in their favor in the judicial mind (which is seldom capable of overcoming its feeling of class solidarity); and by the selection of juries to eliminate "undesirable elements." The special status of political prisoners is difficult or impossible to establish, because those convicted of "political" offenses are almost always opponents of the bourgeois state.

The very administrative services of the state take on the role of coercion and repression. The bureaucracy escapes from the control of those it administers and even from that of their elected representatives. The power vested in it places the state above society; it has become a permanent, unassailable, structured hierarchy objectively at the service of the top layer of the bourgeoisie.

In order to supplant the feudal system and become the dominant class, the bourgeoisie was obliged to call on the mass of people for support. The American Revolution of 1776 and the French Revolution of 1789 are obvious examples. To gain the support of the people, it was necessary to proclaim grandiose principles (the rights of man; equality before the law), and to express demands which established an alliance with the masses. The state proper to capitalism, the democratic republic or *bourgeois democracy* was, from its inception, based on a recognition of rights and freedoms which, in practice, necessarily hindered the accession to power of the new dominant class. The bourgeois republic was obliged to blazon these liberties on its banner, but of necessity strove to limit them for the masses. Hypocrisy was thus one of its essential characteristics.

Historically, the bourgeoisie soon realized that the best way to restrict such rights and liberties for the people was not to reduce or oppose them openly. It was far better to proclaim such rights and liberties for all, while, in practice, seeking to empty most of them of real content. Thus bourgeois democracy proved to be nominal, its practice in relation to the working class continuously in contradiction with its own proclamations.

The liberty proclaimed was illusory for the oppressed class, but nonetheless essential for the bourgeoisie itself. Liberty was really necessary to the bourgeoise for the conquest and defense of its supremacy: it needed freedom of work to acquire the labor power escaping from feudalism; it needed freedom of investment and an end to constraints on trade and the growth of capitalism; it needed the "liberty of the individual" in general, and endowed this with sanctity because it is the ideological justification of private property, the foundation stone of the new mode of production. High principles were used to legitimize private property and enshrine it in the law which was supposedly equal for all. In the name of free enterprise and the right of access to property, the law sanctioned the daily and general misappropriation of a large part of the workers' labor and repressed actions against private property arising from such exploitation.

Bourgeois democracy, the originator of free, compulsory schooling, uses education to imbue the mind of every child, at every age, with the ideology which guarantees the system. The purpose of this is to insure that everyone believes in equality before the law, the benefits of "human" freedom and the moral excellence of a society which denies the interdependence and social responsibility of individuals. Civic instruction and the teaching of literature, history, and philosophy, are all geared to this end. The teaching of practical skills is usually limited to the training of future workers required by the system, conditioning them to fit into their allotted slot. The school system has the further function of perpetuating class divisions, partly by actual social segregation with regard to opportunities for higher studies, and partly by the sharpest possible division between manual and intellectual work, between school and the real world. To add to all this, the content and presentation of teaching material is geared, from start to finish, to the socially privileged children so that selection by apparent aptitude becomes a smokescreen for social selection.

The duplicity of bourgeois democracy is especially apparent in those political fields related to the fundamental issue of national sovereignty.

Freedom of expression and of the press are the recognized right of everyone, but the state does not endow anyone with the means to exercise them. In practice, only those who control the enormous financial resources required enjoy these rights, and those without such means are deprived of them. The dailies and magazines with mass circulations are for the Hearsts and the Loebs and the Luces, while those opposed to the system must make do with mimeographed sheets or, at least, slim publications surviving precariously only through the sacrifices of their supporters.

Freedom of assembly and demonstration are loudly proclaimed, but the state reserves the right to forbid them in the name of public order, and has the police at its disposal to enforce its decision. It is, therefore, not surprising that progressive meetings and demonstrations are constantly impeded by state action and subject to police violence.

Where the radio and television services are state owned, equal time may be measured out to political opponents. However, trendy newscasts, sensationalist dramatic shows, idiotic game shows, and a stupifying flood of advertisements generally add up to a huge antipolitical program in the service of the bourgeoisie—which can only benefit by the political emasculation of its citizens.

Thus, before the act (elections) which is supposed to express national sovereignty where there is a bourgeois democracy, the citizens have been conditioned to accept with favor the propaganda and mystifications of reactionary parties. First they will be told, "You are in a democratic state; anyone who likes can be a candidate; you vote for whoever you like, and your vote is equal to anybody else's."

There are a number of deceptions involved in such persuasion. First, it is untrue that anyone can be a candidate; there has to be a *way* as well as a will. Although some states cover minor expenses, any candidate needs money; the chances of a candidate depend on the ability to spend (on literature, television, and radio time, on advertising and public relations and travel). It follows that any candidate backed by the money of the monopolies is at a great advantage. Second, the electors vote as they wish only insofar as their judgment has survived the general conditioning we have described and the immediate flow of propaganda. In many countries their votes may *not* be equal to those of any other person or persons. Fearful lest all their other direct and indirect pressures may fail, many bourgeois states steal votes by arranging electoral districts so that, for example, 50,000 votes are required to return a representative in a working-class district and only 10,000 in an area which is, by its social structure, expected to return a conservative. Where more than one balloting takes place there is room for other forms of maneuvering, with political groups feigning hostility in the first round in order to produce a reactionary majority and overcome progressive elements in the last.

The myth of mass sovereignty and citizen equality fosters yet another deceit: the state as a just arbiter between classes and social groups. The state (through the government) may be asked to arbitrate certain disputes. To understand this it must be remembered that although the state is the essential element in the superstructure, it is not a passive, automatic reflection of the infrastructure it derives from. Its role is quite specific: to express the power of the dominant class (the capitalists) in all aspects of the organization of social life; and to perform this specific role it requires relative autonomy. Strategically, that is, in the long and medium term, it can only serve the interests of capital, since that is its purpose. Tactically, however, that is in the short term, the state may quite often have to maneuver and even retreat. Bourgeois society is characterized by a class struggle in which the balance of forces is constantly fluctuating. The maneuvers and retreats the state may resort to are not the result of a free judgment in the cause of justice but arise from the need to take into account changes in the balance of forces and to use cunning when it seems unwise to use force.

Changes in bourgeois states since the Second World War show that in their most vital and long-term actions they have not only remained capitalist states, but have become ever more clearly the instruments of large-scale capitalism—*monopoly capitalist states.*

If the bourgeois state was to further the monopolization of the economy, it had to create new methods of intervention. We have seen that it is now able continously to regulate the economy by means such as price fixing, often by determining price levels in agreement with large-scale capitalist bodies; by granting government contracts; by actions bearing on the quantity of money and the distribution of credit; by the regulation of banking activities, etc.

Most usefully, however, the monopoly capitalist state now-adays has the means to act beyond the medium term, and to intervene at the structural level where fundamental and lasting choices are made. It controls the catchment area for a wide range of savings, and a considerable volume of capital which can be put into public or mixed investments which serve as examples and activators to private investors. It has become current practice to directly or indirectly subsidize the economy—that is, the monopolies—and these subsidies provide the necessary restructuring, or redress imbalances between sectors. Arms spending is so specific and extensive that it provides a permanent countercurrent to certain negative tendencies of the system (such as the fall in the rate of profit). The monopoly capitalist state has, finally, taken to planning within the framework of a harmonized or contractual economy and, as far as may be within capitalism, defines the general direction and overall balance of the economy on a medium-term basis. It is the state which concludes external agreements (e.g., as a partner in the European Common Market or other international grouping), which enable the monopolies to prosper in an enlarged economic sphere.

In Europe, as basic transport and energy sectors became less or not at all profitable, the monopoly capitalist state became an employer state and took them over in order to leave the most profitable sectors to large-scale private capital. It even took over pioneer sectors whose main enterprises (atomic energy, aviation, space exploration) require very heavy capital investment and entail high risks but are very stimulating to the economy.

The big capitalist state intervenes directly in the amalgamations of monopolies which accelerate the concentration of capital. Scientific research and development studies require the commitment of considerable sums of capital for uncertain returns. The state undertakes between two-thirds and four-fifths of such expenditure and, moreover, programs financed by public funds are often delegated to monopoly enterprises.

Finally, the monopoly state plays its part to the point of becoming a major banker to the monopolies. The U.S.

government guaranteed a desperately needed loan for defense contractor Lockheed Aircraft, and bailed out the investors and executives of the grossly ill-managed Penn Central railroad.

It is said that the first question a detective asks when out to investigate a crime is: "Who did the crime benefit?" there being a good chance that the beneficiary will turn out to be the instigator of the crime. When we look at the capitalist state we can ask the same question: Who benefits from its actions? And the answer will surely enlighten us about its nature.

The French national accounts for 1971, presented by the state itself, include the following among much other interesting material: between 1959 and 1971 the gross return from exploitation (gross profits of enterprises) rose at an annual rate of 11.3 percent, while average industrial wages rose by 8.4 percent and taxes by 8.8 percent, that is, more slowly than profits, enabling the said companies to increase their savings at a rate of 13 percent per annum.

The capitalist state, however, still sees that company taxes would be an excessive burden, for it allows them to keep a significant part each year as "allowances" for depreciation and depletion. Between 1967 and 1971 the direct taxes paid by French companies amounted to 61.48 billion francs, and 29.43 billion was kept back as "depreciation allowances" which ultimately produce more profit for those same companies.

The above examples from the wealth of evidence available show that the modern state regulates and gives direction to the economy, and generally intervenes in such a way that the fruits of economic growth will be divided so that (a) wage earners and small individual businesses benefit least; (b) medium-sized private companies do better; and (c) the lion's share goes to the giant corporations that can fairly be described as monopolies. The modern state, for its part, certainly merits the title of monopoly capitalist state. This title becomes more and more appropriate as the inequalities we have described continuously grow sharper.

13
Social Classes and the Struggle
Against Capitalism

We have touched on the problems of class in a general way. Now we propose to examine social classes, especially in relation to the struggle against capitalism. We shall not try to present definitive conclusions, but rather to provide material to light the reader's own way into a very complex subject. We shall look at the capitalist classes; then, rather more deeply, at those which earn wages; and then at the intermediate classes. Finally, we shall look at the class struggle in the context of internationalism.

It may seem equivocal to refer to the capitalist classes in the plural. This term is used to cover the monopolistic bourgeoisie and what one might for want of a better term describe as the traditional bourgeoisie—meaning that part which has not joined monopoly capitalism. Both are composed of people who enter into productive relations as owners of the means of production or exchange, and are thus enabled to exploit wage earners and appropriate their surplus labor. From this point of view they together constitute a capitalist class which we can regard as unique. Earlier, however, we saw that the average rate of profit in a given society or country was the average of very different rates of profit enjoyed by different people, and that those whose high rate of profit enables them to preempt the lion's share of total national surplus value can only do so at the expense of the share of others with a lower rate of profit. It is usually the same group, the monopolies, who take most, and the small or medium capitalists who get less. This creates sharp antagonism between these rival contenders for a share of national surplus value. This rivalry is sharpened by the fact that the state is becoming daily more of a monopoly capitalist state, and its interventions in the economy have the ultimate purpose of supporting resistance against the tendency of the rate of profit to fall for the benefit of those best able to resist—the monopolies.

The traditional bourgeoisie recognises its defeat in the competition for the biggest share of surplus value, and sees its only chance of survival in continual growth of the total quantity of surplus value, so that that it may maintain the absolute value of its share of the cake, even though the balance of forces is constantly moving against it. This makes its opposition to the monopolistic bourgeoisie a secondary contradiction, not without significance, but of much less significance than the fundamental contradiction which pits the entire capitalist bourgeoisie (monopolistic and traditional) against all those it exploits: workers and other salaried people. On occasion these workers may, in their struggles, take advantage of internal dissensions in the capitalist class, but we must not forget that all capital holders will ultimately unite against the workers when major confrontations occur.

It must also be remembered that although the traditional bourgeoisie is in competition with the monopolistic bourgeoisie for its share of surplus value, it has become very dependent on the latter's activities. Forced into the role of subcontractors, great numbers of small businesses are increasingly dependent on selling to the giant industries on unfavorable terms. Small-scale producers of consumer goods depend on the large-scale chain stores and distributors to provide outlets for their products. These relationships, as well as dependence on banking credit, all contribute to bringing the traditional bourgeoisie into the shadow of the monopolies and turning it into an underdeveloped, backward sector of the economy.

A concrete examination of the wage-earning classes requires some appreciation of their numbers. In the United States in 1975 the employed population amounted to 78.3 million persons, broken down as shown in the table below.

Table 1
(in millions of persons)

Agriculture	1.3
Construction, mining, and manufacturing	22.5
Transportation and public utilities	4.5
Trade and finance	21.2
Services	14.0
Government	14.8
Total	78.3

Source: *Employment and Training Report of the President* (Washington, D.C.: Government Printing Office, 1976).

Domestic and agricultural workers in advanced capitalist societies are often too scattered and too few in number to play any great anticapitalist role. Many agricultural workers are, moreover, only temporary workers; we shall therefore leave them out of the ensuing argument.

Marxist analysis has always stressed the distinction between *productive* and *nonproductive* workers. The former are exclusively wage earners (otherwise called direct producers), whose labor produces *value* and, especially, the additional or surplus value appropriated by the capitalist and constituting the return on capital. We saw earlier that only the production of commodities, that is, material goods with an exchange value, can give rise to new surplus value. Thus, productive workers are those who produce such material goods and collectively constitute the *working class.*

The groups of workers indicated in the above statistics are large and imprecise. The heading, "Construction, mining, and manufacturing," comprises both the mass of unskilled workers and the supervisory and office staff in these sectors. On the other hand, it does not include transport workers (especially the truck drivers) and others engaged in productive activity. Taking this into account one may estimate that the U.S. working class (excluding farm workers) now contains about 28 million workers, or about 40 percent of all wage and salary earners. However, this working class is now growing slightly less rapidly than all other categories of employed persons combined. This change, however, is slow moving and most likely the working class, compared to other employed groups, will continue to be the largest unit of wage and salary workers.

The working class has, moreover, always been the vanguard, which is believed to follow from the fact that it is composed of direct producers. The exploitation arising from capitalist productive relations certainly affects these workers most brutally and immediately; the major pressure to extract surplus value impinges directly on them. For these reasons, and also because of its concentration in large productive units, the working class is the collective worker *par excellence*. It inherits traditions of mighty social struggles. It continues not only to be numerically the most important sector of the salaried population, but potentially its most conscious and coherent element.

This does not obviate the fact that workers are subject to the pressure of the dominant ideology, and not immune from the poison of the consumer society. The quantitative improvement in workers' standards of living sometimes blunts their will to fight. Their homogeneity is undermined by skill differentials and training. Nevertheless, some observers have exaggerated the importance of these factors. Our first comment is that ideological pressure, rising living standards, and all kinds of divisive tactics affect not only the working class, but every class and type of wage earner. Each of these harbors a contradiction between its specific consciousness and the ideological onslaught of the dominant class. For various reasons, moreover, within each group there arise secondary contradictions and conflicts which the dominant class is not slow to inflame—if it did not indeed provoke them. Finally, we know that in recent years working-class groups all over the world have undertaken the most strenuous actions which put its militancy above question. Moreover, in various struggles priority has often been given to demands for the improvement of the lowest wages which demonstrates a spirit of solidarity despite all efforts to create disunity by the proliferation of work categories. It is likewise undeniable that solidarity between the bulk of the working class and specially underprivileged minority group workers has increased, although earlier hindered by a racist taint created and maintained by the dominant class. To sum up, it is still the working class which conducts the most numerous, determined and effective anticapitalist actions. The battle must still be waged in its name in the knowledge that its role must be decisive.

This does not mean that groups of wage earners classed as *nonproductive workers* may not play an important supporting role. These nonproductive workers are growing in numbers slightly faster than is the working class. The nonproductive workers in private trade, in service, and in financial institutions already number close on 5 million. Their very numbers call for our attention, and other considerations require that their case be seriously examined.

If one uses the term *commercial employee* in the widest sense to include those in advertising, market research, etc., the great majority of nonproductive workers are to be found in this group; moreover, an analysis of their case can be extrapolated to most of the service industries and financial institutions—that is, to the tertiary sector. Marxist analysis is still elementary in this field, so we turn to Marx himself: "The commercial worker produces no surplus value directly. . . ." In fact it is the function of commerce on the one hand to *realize* the surplus value contained in the merchandise by converting it into money and, on the other, to create the necessary conditions for *increas-*

ing this surplus value by accelerating the circulation of capital. To do this commercial capital is allocated part of the surplus value realized. But, Marx adds, "The price of his [the commercial worker's] labour is determined by the value of his labour power . . . , while the application of this labour-power, its exertion, expenditure of energy, and wear and tear is, as in the case of every other wage earner by no means limited by its value."[1] Like industrial workers, the commercial worker "performs partly unpaid labour"[2] and in the final analysis:

> Just as the labourer's unpaid labour directly creates surplus value for productive capital, so the unpaid labour of the commercial wage-worker secures a share of this surplus value for the merchant's capital. . . .which amounts to the same thing [as surplus value], with respect to his capital.[3]

These quotations blaze the trail for a clear analysis: where productive relations are concerned, there is no fundamental difference between the directly productive worker and the nonproductive worker who nevertheless contributes to the accumulation of capital: their exploitation is essentially the same. As Marx put it, "In one respect such a commercial employee is a wage-worker like any other."[4] It is true that, in certain other ways, he or she differs from an industrial worker, but these are not relevant to the nature of exploitation. Marx noted that in his time the "commercial worker . . . belongs to the better-paid class of wage-earners."[5]

He then adds that "the labour-power of these people is therefore devaluated with the progress of capitalist production. Their wage falls while their labour capacity increases."[6] This development has continued, until in our time commercial employees without special training are among the most exploited. Sociological differences nonetheless exist: there are blue-collar and white-collar workers. Commercial employees and those in the tertiary sector generally are more scattered than factory workers, and less conscious of being part of a class. They lack the tradition of great industrial and social struggles. But these are differences in secondary characteristics or are in the process of changing. Some recent hard-fought strikes by commercial employees show that this change is progressing.

Thus nonproductive workers who contribute to the accumulation of capital properly belong in the ranks of those struggling against capitalism. Together with the industrial working class they constitute what Marx defined as the *proletariat*, that is, all the workers whose labor "increases capital."

There are other nonproductive workers who do not contribute to the accumulation of capital and who must be considered with greater reserve. This is the case with the numerically important group of administrative employees. This category does not include those employed in productive state enterprises: energy, transport, etc. These latter belong to the working class as producers of surplus value. The fact that their employer is a public body does not change the capitalist nature of the productive relations to which they are subject.

Administrative employees, moreover, vary greatly. One important group is the teachers (who will be discussed when we come to consider the intellectuals). Employees in postal and telecommunications are another large group. They are employed by the state in autonomous bodies mainly economic in character whose services bring in a return. Some of these wage earners are manual workers and others not, and their position is hard to define. They have been known to present collective, firm opposition to the exploitation affecting them and, in the final analysis, they seem to be closer to commercial employees than to those of the state administration.

With the exception of the above two groups, employees of the state administration at all levels are all to a greater or lesser degree subject to the direct ideological and political pressure of the capitalist state. At the lower- and middle-income levels their labor power is just as fully exploited as that of commercial employees, but they are often imbued with a sense of their role as representatives of the capitalist state which, in turn, shows them that they are a special and separate group by giving them lifelong contracts. It follows that these people only take part marginally and episodically in the anticapitalist struggle.

We cannot overlook the two groups of wage earners who are most talked about: the intellectuals and the "middle management." The idea of *middle management* seems to be inseparable from that of hierarchy and authority. Middle management personnel are private employees placed at a specific point of articulation within an enterprise to exercise authority delegated by management—that is, by capital. Their wages are composed of a part representing the value of their labor power and another part taken from surplus value to reward them for their services as agents of capital. In these circumstances supervisory staff cannot identify with the anticapitalist struggle, though there may be a few individual exceptions. On occasion a secondary contradiction may bring them into conflict with capital in regard to the extent of their authority within an enterprise, but this does not affect their capitalist character. Even when sections of this group seem to lend a favorable ear to some notions of socialism we should remain skeptical. Do they not conceive of socialism simply as a system which would establish them as the top bureaucracy—that is, the opposite of socialism?

The *intellectual worker* is one whose labor power is based entirely on mental labor. He or she is not to be identified with the supervisor—usually also endowed with intelligence—because the intellectual neither holds nor transmits any fraction of capital's authority. The difference lies in their functions. The identical engineer is a supervisor if he or she is integrated into a production process, but becomes an intellectual worker if assigned to research. Within an enterprise this intellectual worker is a productive worker, for: "In order to labour productively, it is enough, if you are an organ of the collective labourer, and perform one of its subordinate functions."[7] The argument which enabled us to identify the commercial employee with the industrial wage earner is equally valid for an intellectual worker in an nonproductive sector serving the accumulation of capital. Intellectual workers who sell nothing but their labor power are not numerous, and usually function in small dispersed groups (the exceptions being national research establishments and atomic energy agencies). They lack cohesion and though they often join the anticapitalist struggle as individuals, a number of individual decisions do not necessarily lead to collective participation. The main potential role of such people is educational and inspirational.

Teachers are in a different situation. They are mostly state employed and play no part in production or the accumulation of capital, but they play a role in creating the labor power of the workers who become their pupils, increasing their value by the social element of a higher qualification. Thus their function is not comparable with others in the pay of the state who are office employees in public administration. They enjoy much greater independence in the exercise of their functions. Finally, by their numbers and cohesion and by the respect and consideration they usually enjoy, they constitute a unique social group whose lower ranks are severely exploited by the capitalist state. Within the general struggle against capitalism the action appropriate to teachers is not by its nature likely gravely to threaten the system, because it does not strike at its vital organs. Such action, nevertheless, has a particular significance if only because it affects every family in the country.

The *intermediate classes* are varied but not very numerous and in the United States in 1975 the active nonsalaried population was broken down as shown in Table 2.

A wide variety of activities are included here. Although big capitalists are found in both groups, the self-employed are essentially either small- or medium-sized farmers, owners of small business establishments (retail stores or services businesses, including beauty parlors, barber shops, laundries, funeral parlors, etc.), or professionals (lawyers, doctors, accountants).

Table 2
(in millions of persons)

Self-employed in agriculture	1.7
Self-employed in nonagricultural occupations	5.6
Total	7.3

Source: *Employment and Training Report of the President* (Washington, D.C.: Government Printing Office, 1976).

Small businesses have become very unstable since shopping centers, giant retail chain stores, and service chains such as dry cleaning and auto repair have been set up everywhere, taking an increasing share of trade. The large-scale entry of big capital into the retailing and service industries has created serious problems for merchants of modest means. Thus small traders are falling prey to the giants, but this does not prevent the two from being members of the group sharing in surplus value. The interest of the retailers vis à vis the worker-consumers can only be the fierce defense of their margin of profit, that is, their share of surplus value. The interest of the worker-consumers, on the other hand, is to undermine all kinds of surplus value (industrial and commercial profit, etc.) in the hope that overall surplus value will thereby be more easily reduced and their exploitation lessened. Retailers and service people as a class thus cannot be fundamental allies of the workers in the anticapitalist struggle. At best, in a tactical sense, the anticapitalist struggle may have an interest in exploiting the secondary contradiction between small businesses and big capital, while recalling that it may become a *primary* contradiction for those small retailers who are eliminated and thus "proletarianized."

Small and medium farmers have fallen sharply in numbers through the proletarianization of those whose holdings were no longer viable, but they are still a numerous group whose decline will come to an end. In less than twenty years, from 1950 to 1969, the number of farms in the United States declined by half—from 5.4 to 2.7 million. This was not due to a decline in agricultural activity, but resulted from the rapid process of concentration of U.S. agriculture into large-scale capitalist enterprise. Thus in 1969 a little over 2 percent of U.S. farms consisted of at least 2,000 acres. And these large farms accounted for 40 percent of U.S. farmland. At the other end of the scale, 23 percent of the farms in 1969 were less than 50 acres, and another 17 percent were between 50 and 99 acres. Taken together, these two groups—or 40 percent of the farms—operated less than 100 acres each and accounted for less than 5 percent of total farmland. In France in 1970-1971 there were just under 1,600,000 agricultural holdings, 70 percent of which were of less than twenty hectares and 22 percent between twenty and fifty hectares.

Such small-scale farmers are commodity producers, but are not directly controlled by the capitalist mode of production. The farmers own their own means of production. However, as Marx observed, "means of production become capital only insofar as . . . they confront labour"—which is not the case for the farmers, who are their own labor. Marx held that such people create surplus value and appropriate it themselves solely because the ownership of their means of production enables them to take possession of their own surplus labor. It is clear, however, that Marx's comment was based on a period when most farmers bought almost nothing and produced everything on their own, with the exception of land and instruments of labor. Today most farmers do not produce their own energy (draft animals), their seeds, tools, or other supplies. They have become dependent on the market for everything antecedent to their actual production and are equally dependent on the market for everything subsequent to it, for they now sell almost all their products. The market for their input is dominated by agricultural machinery monopolies, those controlling fertilizer and chemical products, etc., and the market for their output is controlled by the monopoly state, which fixes or directs most prices. Thus gripped in a vice, today's small-scale farmer is in some sense a sort of home worker for a collective employer which is none other than monopoly itself. The question remains whether farmers now take possession of their own surplus labor or whether it is appropriated by the system.

In any case many farmers (or peasants) around the world have analyzed their position broadly, and as a class have shown themselves capable of conducting violent and determined anticapitalist struggles with a strong sense of solidarity with the working class.

Our brief analysis of class is relevant not just to conditions within one society, but to relationships which spread across the globe. The multinational companies through which monopoly capital is developing everywhere behave in the same way in every latitude. General Electric will certainly have no more tender concern for its new South Korean or Brazilian workers, or for those of a dozen other countries, than it had for its workers in the United States. The Chase Manhattan Bank will pursue profit just as fiercely in Europe, Asia, Africa, or South America as it does in North America. What is clear is that workers everywhere have no recourse but to struggle against their exploitation by capital—and that the very development of monopoly capitalism can only make workers more and more conscious of this necessity.

Lack of space prevents us from entering into a full discussion on internationalism here, but it cannot be ignored. It would be a betrayal of the truth to permit readers to imagine any capitalist society bounded simply within national frontiers. A national reality exists which is still more than an empty concept, but beyond and in spite of it international class stratification stretches across the entire capitalist world and transcends all frontiers.

The increasing monopolization of capital is universal and is everywhere achieved by the same methods: the fundamental interests and purposes of monopoly capitalism are the same in every quarter of the globe. International associations of monopolistic capital which were formerly slow to take shape have in recent years become more common in the most varied forms. In France the main banks have entered into international association with those of other big capitalist countries (cf. in Germany Crédit Lyonnais is called Commerzbank) and the premier finance bank, the Cie. Financière de Paris et Les Pays-Bas in 1972 entered into an important association with one of Britain's biggest banks. The big capitalist class (already at the monopoly level or striving to achieve it) everywhere aspires to establish an international order which will eliminate national differences. It is becoming a *world bourgeoisie* in pursuit of a unity essential for its major purposes, whatever internal contradictions it may experience. In almost all the so-called Third World countries this imperialist world bourgeoisie takes in as minor partners the local bourgeoisie or privileged commercial and bureaucratic elements which can subjugate and exploit their own workers only in partnership with imperialism.

The increasing universality of the world bourgeoisie implies an increased objective universality of all those who produce surplus value for it. This means the growth of what can be defined as a *world proletariat*, uniting those who contribute to the accumulation of capital wherever they may be. It may seem surprising to put a Detroit autoworker and an African grower of coffee or peanuts into the same category of world proletariat; in the framework of a world market dominated by monopoly capital, however, both are participants in the expanding reproduction of capital, even though the former produces surplus value directly and the other is exploited by unequal exchange and other means. Do not the African or Asian growers experience this identity when, driven out of plantations or holdings which cannot produce enough to feed their workers, they find themselves transformed into workers on a European conveyor belt within a few weeks?

There is a growing awareness of the international solidarity of workers which follows from the conception of a world bourgeoisie and a world proletariat. On several occasions different trade union groups have expressed this solidarity not only at the organizational level but by the international coordination of struggle. In October 1972 a major liberal French daily paper asserted in a headline that external proletarian support had given a French strike *international dimensions.* Within European nations this solidarity finds expression in increasing solidarity between immigrant and indigenous workers; elsewhere it finds expression in a multitude of ways. But we must realize that a great deal yet remains to be done before a true international proletarian consciousness can arise.

14
General Alienation:
An Increasingly Irrational System

Marx has written that "it is a characteristic feature of labour which posits exchange-value that it causes the social relations of individuals to appear in the perverted form of a social relation between things."[1] From the moment commodity A is exchanged for commodity B on the market, both appear as protagonists in a relationship of things which masks the social relations between their respective producers. This relation between things, between objects, takes on a fantastic and mystifying form; commodities take on the characteristics of "fetishes," giving the false impression of an existence independent of the workers who produced them and the conditions of their production.

This "commodity fetishism" leads directly to money fetishism, since money is that special commodity or general equivalent without which no exchange can be transacted. Thus money fetishism is only a higher and more abstract form of commodity fetishism. According to Marx, as production is more completely transformed into commodity production, producers increasingly need and desire to become merchants, in order to obtain money for their products or for their services, when these are the only products they have to offer. From that point, *making money* becomes the ultimate aim of all activity. As early as 1861, Marx perceived the fact that in a capitalist system money becomes the beacon to which people rush like moths to a candle—a perception which has extraordinary resonance in our day.

The fetishism of money leads us naturally to the phenomenon described as *alienation*. The concept is widely held, yet disputed by some. It is the more easily grasped in that for Marx himself the mode of production based on exchange value "creates an alienation of the individual from himself and from others, but also for the first time the general and universal nature of his relationships and capacities."[2]

Thus Marx had an extensive interpretation of alienation ranging from the economic sphere to the ideological and political; but he certainly paid the closest attention to the fundamental alienation of the wage earner.

Under this heading the sense of the term "alienation" is not far from "exploitation" and "oppression." But it is richer in meaning, adding the very specific idea conveyed by words like "dispossession," "spoliation," or "deprivation." Wage earners are despoiled of the instruments of production, and those they use are the property of the capitalist who buys their labor power. They are dispossessed of the material product of their labor, for the objects they produce or hope to produce are in no way their property. They are deprived of part of the value produced by their labor, their surplus labor appearing only as surplus value for capital that is not theirs. They are even separated from the conditions of labor, for

labour is a totality—*a combination of kinds of labour*—of which the individual constituents are alien to each other, so that the total labour is not the achievement of individual workers, and their product is only a totality through the enforced combination of efforts that they cannot themselves coordinate. In this combination, labour serves an alien will and an alien intelligence; it is they who direct it.[3]

There could be no better description of the robot worker under the industrial system of mass production and the subdivision of tasks. Workers become totally alienated—

having sold, like any other commodity, the only thing about them in which capitalists are interested, their labour power. They are then nothing more than a "source of energy," as powerless and lacking in personality as the fuel or electricity used by those same capitalists. But one thing does distinguish them: this source of energy is endowed with intelligence. It follows on the one hand that the worker's hand commanded by a brain is an irreplaceable tool, for even in the most manual and repetitive task he or she reacts if anything goes wrong. It follows even more inevitably that the worker who is moreover a human being becomes aware of the alienation and, by opposing it, shows the capitalist that he or she is unalterably other than the mere source of energy which the capitalist desires.

One could describe this alienation as *infrastructural*, because it operates at the level of the economic infrastructure which constitutes the capitalist mode of production and appeared at the same historical time as that mode of production itself. It has given rise to violent protests against increasing subdivision of industrial tasks, inhuman work rates, and in general the organization of work as if a worker were nothing more than a machine.

Capitalist alienation, however, affects more than the infrastructure—or at any rate more than immediate production—especially in the present day. In some passages Marx seems to set free time against working time in the capitalist system, as though leisure gave the worker an opportunity to escape and develop his or her personality. It is true that until fairly recently capitalist productive relations did not extend beyond the factory gate, so that outside it the worker felt that he or she was more or less beyond their grasp. A considerable part of the workers' means of subsistence came from noncapitalist sectors. The individual garden combined the advantage of supplying part of their needs while enabling them to function as individuals. While leisure activities were fewer than today, a worker had a greater sense of indulging his or her inclinations within the framework of closer human relations.

It does not require a long exposition to show that, especially since the Second World War, capitalist productive relations and their extensions no longer govern the worker only during the eight hours of contracted daily labor, but rather for twenty-four hours out of the twenty-four. To the basic alienation of the worker as producer has been added the alienation of the worker as consumer, and the alienation of the worker as citizen—that is, alienation by the state—becomes increasingly intolerable. To sum up, capitalism, formerly described as essentially a mode of production, has become ever more clearly a mode of production closely and unavoidably linked to a mode of living.

The reasons are basically economic. Monopoly capitalists are engaged in a difficult struggle against the tendency for the rate of profit to fall, are determined to maintain the fastest possible rate of capital accumulation. They dare not leave fallow any field that might possibly yield profit.

In order to increase the total volume of profit when the rate is difficult to maintain, it is necessary to break in wherever they had not previously penetrated—to violate family life, to present for every need an article or service contributing to extended reproduction of capital or, if the needs presented are too few, to create new ones. For monopoly capitalism the development of the productive forces on the basis of constantly growing consumption is not an option but an absolute economic imperative. We are witnessing a disruption of ways of life and, ultimately, of civilization. This is in no way an independent or natural cultural development, but the direct result of the historic development of the capitalist mode of production. It is nonetheless true that the relations between human beings and commodities are rapidly replacing people-to-people relations, or, to use Marx's simple and terrible expression, "commodities appear as buyers of persons."

Commodities really buy persons in the sense that the new capitalism can only perpetuate itself by devoting ever more capital to buying labor power for the hypertrophied segments of the tertiary sector and other parasitic activities. This arises from an internal logic which, paradoxically, develops with increasing irrationality. We have seen that

the resources committed to distribution and more generally the tertiary sector are simply false costs of the
system—subsidiary expenditures which, unlike those of the
productive sector, do not create surplus value. Yet these
false costs are increasingly unavoidable in a situation of
sharpening competition because they speed up the circulation of capital invested in production and indirectly contribute to increasing the total volume of surplus value
produced in a given time—an increase ultimately greater
than the share of surplus value consumed by these activities. The fall in the rate of profit is thus checked.

In this way consumer society is organized to direct an
ever increasing share of available labor power and capital
not to the production of more useful commodities but to
auxiliary activities of doubtful value whose sole purpose
is to activate the distribution of the quantities of consumer
goods produced, be they useful or useless. This serves to
accelerate the realization of the surplus value they con-
tain and increase the resulting profits. The system which
sees itself as devoted to production for profit is constrained
to divert ever more workers and capital from production
into valueless activities, even though enormous potential
—and greatly needed production—is ignored in the unprof-
itable fields of urban and rural renewal, the environment,
education, culture, health, sport, and social purposes generally. Thus irrationality triumphs and the life forces of
society are wasted.

Even the least conscious sections of the public eventually become more or less aware of this waste. On each
half-hour television program one encounters five or six
housewives of the small screen, successively lauding five
or six detergents which usually differ only in name. The
public begins to think, quite rightly, "We are paying for
all this!" On further reflection people become aware of
the enormous waste. They begin to imagine a society
which, without advertisements, would make available a
single detergent for each given purpose—the best and the
cheapest.

Parasitic activities come to prey on real productive activities. New needs can be artificially created, and a perpetual evolution stimulated from preexistent needs to new forms of products. The obsolescence of consumer goods is planned and predetermined so that what gave perfect satisfaction up to the present suddenly appears imperfect and outdated in comparison with the new product advertised—but which really contains only new gadgets and trimmings. However, it causes new machine tools to be put into the factories, and equipment and production lines to be modified. The Gross National Product will rise, as will gross profits, but what effect will all this have on the sum of national happiness?

Consumer capitalism constantly violates the private being of the consumer, but can only succeed if the violation is disguised as a free gift of the self. The system can only get at the consumers' pocketbooks by violating their consciousness. It may be an overstatement that this requires the creation of a new ideology, but at least there is required a constellation of mental reactions which causes the victims not only to accept their fate, but to hasten toward it. Freedom is elevated to a high pedestal so that consumers, or rather citizen-consumers, will be able to exercise their freedom with the minimum of cerebral effort; they only have to choose between twenty or thirty detergents; between ten or fifteen cars with identical virtues and possibilities; between two or three predigested answers to a political or commercial questionnaire; between fifty package holidays with fixed prices and programs; between candidate X and candidate Y in a presidential election. The opportunities to exercise this false freedom continue to multiply, reducing freedom to a choice between imposed alternatives. It is forbidden to reason, reflect, or exercise the imagination; but you, the universal roulette player, are entitled to a free choice between the red and the black.

With the restoration of liberty we are to expect a return of happiness, but not that vague concept of happiness to which we earlier referred. It will be a concrete, solid happiness reflected in the appearance on the market of an ever increasing variety of easily consumed goods and services in ever greater quantity. Thus economic growth will be worshipped, substituted for patriotic feeling, and made the measure of civilization and progress, it being taken for granted, or even reaffirmed, that national prosperity will naturally be equitably distributed among all citizens.

One could go on. But we simply want to highlight the ideological and political conditioning of all citizens—who are also the customers essential to the expansion of consumer capitalism, which is equally monopoly capitalism. This conditioning is now taking place at quantitative and qualitative levels until recently unimaginable, and is creating a type of alienation which can be termed *superstructural,* in contrast to what we earlier described as infrastructural. These alienations affect the consciousness, feelings, customs, and idea structures of human beings, and alter their rights and their roles. In the long run, they impinge upon the whole direction and meaning people want to give to their lives.

It is the task of the capitalist state, that specialist in falsification, to use the methods of advertising to convince alienated citizens that they are, more than ever before, free citizens in a free society. While power is being concentrated in the hands of monopoly capital and the monopoly state, it is essential to affirm that, by the politics of so-called participation everyone has free access to all decisions. As the share of big capital in the results of expansion increases, so does its interest in proving to the workers that they have access to the fruits of their labor. The monopoly state sees the sharpening of the fundamental contradiction within the bourgeois state: it must speak of freedom, while at the same time the condition for greater accumulation of capital is an end to freedom; it must hail the power of the people, while resorting to electoral fraud; to maintain the power of big capital it must pay lip service to local control although unequal development is a rule of capitalism and the exercise of power to the benefit of the monopolies requires a more and more centralized state. It must appear to be organizing harmonious development and safeguarding the natural environment, while in reality the maximization of profit and the dictatorship of the commodity market are the cause of headlong urbanization, widespread pollution, and so on.

Waves of aggression, conditioning, lies, and propaganda buffet the citizens-producers-consumers about like straws in the wind, and their reactions are usually ambiguous and even contradictory. On the one hand, they are the often willing victims of superstructural alienations which promote a kind of passive comfort. On the other hand, however confused they may be, the effect is ultimately suffocating and deforming. The very person who was provoked by idiotic television advertising to protest, "It is we who pay for it," might yet feel deprived if one day it were to be missing. It is the daily dose of a poison which has become familiar. Those who denounce the civilization of the car will bow down to the private car; indeed, many could not easily do without one in a country where public transport is inadequate. These same persons may surprise themselves by showing the reactions of alienated people when they are at the wheel.

These superstructural alienations impinge on every individual life at every hour of every day, creating a contradiction between submission and protest, of which the dominant element will change from situation to situation and individual to individual. It is clear, however, that protest is everywhere on the increase. Its expressions are increasingly militant, sometimes violent, and it is producing collective actions. At the same time it takes but little to move the coercive state from oppression to brutal repression.

The most obvious weapon of the state is the bludgeon of the so-called forces of law and order; the state wears its police forces like armor. But these police cannot stem the alarming growth of delinquency and crime, social disintegration, and the dawning consciousness that society as a whole may be on the road to world disaster. In the meantime the scientists are achieving marvels so that human beings feel more and more masters and possessors of nature, but possessors who have lost possession of their own lives.

In the previous chapter we analyzed social classes in terms of their place in productive relations. This analysis remains fundamental, but is not the only one. Motivations arising from so-called superstructural alienation are playing a rapidly increasing part in challenges to the system and struggles against capitalism.

These motivations are not simply in addition to those arising from the exploitation of labor, but interact with them. Individual productive workers will be more or less militant at their workplace as they are more or less resistent to the lures and mystifications of the consumer society. Their awareness of the exploitation of their labor will be reinforced by their understanding of the malfunction of the whole society, and vice-versa. The same applies even more emphatically when we consider social classes and groups rather than individuals. We have already seen protest actions in which the fight against material exploitation was inextricably mixed with the revolt against authoritarianism. This highlights the value of a comprehensive analysis and, equally, of political education, for greater awareness rarely occurs spontaneously. In recent years a new phenomenon has appeared: superstructural alienation has given rise to the adoption of an anticapitalist stance by individuals and social groups who had not until then been sufficiently motivated by the capitalist exploitation of their labor. Superstructural alienation in all its forms has penetrated the entire fabric of society. It brings groups which are especially sensitive to it into the anticapitalist camp, and strengthens other classes and groups already committed to the struggle. While we must not exaggerate its effects, it would be a mistake to overlook the fact that small reinforcements can sometimes upset the balance of forces.

15
Conclusion:
Where Do We Go from Here?

Our conclusion is brief, since it is already inherent in our text. Two points will suffice. First, the capitalist system represents one historic moment in the evolution of modes of production and human society. At one period it set free the energy for an enormous development of productive forces and human activities. Later its internal contradictions became a barrier to this development, insofar as it purported to satisfy the needs and aspirations of humankind. It was certainly an advance on previous systems; but it is now itself an obstacle on the way to that higher social order which has become necessary to humankind.

Second, this higher social order—socialism—is thus not an abstract concept produced solely by the imagination. On the one hand it is born of capitalism and destined to be its heir; on the other it can and must be its negation. It would be adventuristic and dangerous to offer a conception of socialism on any basis but this fundamental contradiction and the necessary task of overcoming it.

For this reason there is an essential prerequisite for any study of socialism and for the search for ways to achieve the transition: this is the most scientific analysis possible of the capitalist mode of production and the society to which it has given rise.

This book was conceived as an introduction to such a study. Many readers will, rightly, want to learn more. What advice can we give them?

First let us turn to Marx himself—to his essential writings in increasing order of difficulty. Begin with *The Communist Manifesto* (1848); then go on to *Wages, Price and Profit* (1865); and then make a frontal attack on *Capital* (1867). We must admit that this reading is arduous and calls for a real effort. So we recommend readers to proceed empirically, taking it in small doses. We even suggest interrupting the reading of *Capital* by turning to Engels' pamphlet *Socialism: Utopian and Scientific* and by reading Lenin, who has the advantage of being generally easy to follow. Lenin's works should preferably be read in the following order: *State and Revolution* (1917); *Imperialism: The Highest Stage of Capitalism* (1917); *What Is to Be Done?* (1902).

Marxism does not stop at the works of Marx, Engels, and Lenin, but these are universal, while the writings of their successors have been turned into holy texts for far too many sects. So we shall stay with the three indisputably great names for what is a first approach—with one additional comment. Those who want to initiate a study of the philosophy, which is an essential element of Marxism, could not do better than begin with the still unsurpassed work of Georges Politzer: *Elementary Principles of Philosophy* (1946).

It is self-evident that these fundamental works must always be studied within the social and historical context of the periods and countries in which they were written. This is especially important for the works of Lenin, whose writing was always closely linked to concrete situations for specific events.

Marxism is a science of reality and of human society; it is applied to changing and evolving data in order to formulate the permanent principles and general laws governing them. Through the application of these laws, Marxism enables us to perceive the economic regularities inherent in human society. This means that the laws indicate general directions, but their movement may be checked in any given situation. Marxism is incompatible with all forms of linear or mechanistic determinism. Indeed, its very essence is dialectic and its most unique contribution is the study of the confrontation of contradictory elements and forces and the analysis of their balance. Thus Marxism as a science calls for a separate analysis of each new situation, taking basic laws and principles as a starting point. Marxism is by its very nature *antidogmatic*.

Notes

Chapter 2. Production: How and With What?
1. Karl Marx, *Capital*, Vol. I (New York: International Publishers, 1967), p. 714.
2. Ibid., p. 44.
3. *Marx-Engels Selected Works* (Moscow: Foreign Languages Publishing House, 1951), p. 379.

Chapter 4. Labor Power: A Unique Commodity
that Creates Surplus Value
1. Karl Marx, *Capital*, Vol. I (New York: International Publishers, 1967), p. 167.
2. Ibid., p. 171.
3. Delaunay, *Essai marxiste sur la comptabilité nationale* (Paris: Editions Sociales, 1971), p. 87.

Chapter 6. Profit: The Rolling Stone that Gathers Moss
1. Karl Marx, *Capital*, Vol. III (New York: International Publishers, 1967), p. 43.

Chapter 7. Profit in Various Guises
1. Karl Marx, *Capital*, Vol. III (New York: International Publishers, 1967), p. 392.

Chapter 11. Monopoly Power: The New Face of Imperialism
1. This chapter was written a few months before the oil-producing countries of the Middle East declared the "petroleum war" in the autumn of 1973. This was a glaring illustration of the vital dependence of the imperialist countries on raw materials from Third World countries and of the latter's resistance to imperialist domination.

Chapter 13. Social Classes and the Struggle Against Capitalism
1. Karl Marx, *Capital*, Vol. III (New York: International Publishers, 1967), p. 300.
2. Ibid.
3. Ibid., p. 294.
4. Ibid., p. 292.
5. Ibid., p. 300.
6. Ibid., pp. 300-01.
7. Ibid., Vol. I, pp. 508-09

Chapter 14. General Alienation: An Increasingly
Irrational System
1. Karl Marx, *A Contribution to the Critique of Political Economy* (New York: International Publishers, 1971), p. 34.
2. Marx, *Grundrisse*, edited by D. McLellan (New York: Harper, 1971), p. 71.
3. Ibid., p. 117.